ANCIENT ROME

ANCIENT ROME

Other books in this series include:

Ancient Egypt
Ancient Greece
The Civil War
The Middle Ages
The Native Americans

ANCIENT ROME

DON NARDO

LUCENT BOOKS®

THOMSON
™
GALE

San Diego • Detroit • New York • San Francisco • Cleveland • New Haven, Conn. • Waterville, Maine • London • Munich

THOMSON
GALE

On cover: The siege of Alesia, 52 B.C. by Henri Paul Motte.

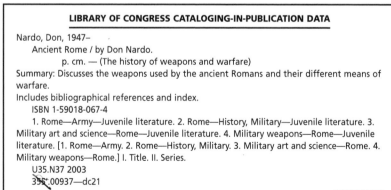

LIBRARY OF CONGRESS CATALOGING-IN-PUBLICATION DATA

Nardo, Don, 1947–
    Ancient Rome / by Don Nardo.
        p. cm. — (The history of weapons and warfare)
Summary: Discusses the weapons used by the ancient Romans and their different means of warfare.
Includes bibliographical references and index.
    ISBN 1-59018-067-4
    1. Rome—Army—Juvenile literature. 2. Rome—History, Military—Juvenile literature. 3. Military art and science—Rome—Juvenile literature. 4. Military weapons—Rome—Juvenile literature. [1. Rome—Army. 2. Rome—History, Military. 3. Military art and science—Rome. 4. Military weapons—Rome.] I. Title. II. Series.
    U35.N37 2003
    355.00937—dc21

                         2002006601

Printed in the U.S.A.

Contents

FOREWORD   8

INTRODUCTION   10
Rome's Unique Approach to Warfare

CHAPTER ONE   14
The Early Roman Army

CHAPTER TWO   28
The Development of Manipular Tactics

CHAPTER THREE   43
The Professional Imperial Military Forces

CHAPTER FOUR   60
Fortifications and Siege Warfare

CHAPTER FIVE   75
Naval Weapons and Tactics

CHAPTER SIX   88
The Decline and Fall of Rome's Military

LEGIONS OF THE EARLY EMPIRE   102
DISTRIBUTION OF THE LEGIONS A.D. 23 TO 138   105
NOTES   107
GLOSSARY   110
FOR FURTHER READING   114
MAJOR WORKS CONSULTED   115
ADDITIONAL WORKS CONSULTED   119
INDEX   121
PICTURE CREDITS   127
ABOUT THE AUTHOR   128

Foreword

The earliest battle about which any detailed information has survived took place in 1274 B.C. at Kadesh, in Syria, when the armies of the Egyptian and Hittite empires clashed. For this reason, modern historians devote a good deal of attention to Kadesh. They know that this battle and the war of which it was a part were not the first fought by the Egyptians and their neighbors. Many other earlier conflicts are mentioned in ancient inscriptions found throughout the Near East and other regions, as from the dawn of recorded history city-states fought one another for political or economic dominance.

Moreover, it is likely that warfare long predated city-states and written records. Some scholars go so far as to suggest that the Cro-Magnons, the direct ancestors of modern humans, wiped out another early human group—the Neanderthals—in a prolonged and fateful conflict in the dim past. Even if this did not happen, it is likely that even the earliest humans engaged in conflicts and battles over territory and other factors. "Warfare is almost as old as man himself," writes renowned military historian John Keegan, "and reaches into the most secret places of the human heart, places where self dissolves rational purpose, where pride reigns, where emotion is paramount, where instinct is king."

Even after humans became "civilized," with cities, writing, and organized religion, the necessity of war was widely accepted. Most people saw it as the most natural means of defending territory, maintaining security, or settling disputes. A character in a dialogue by the fourth-century B.C. Greek thinker Plato declares:

> All men are always at war with one another. . . . For what men in general term peace is only a name; in reality, every city is in a natural state of war with every other, not indeed proclaimed by heralds, but everlasting. . . . No possessions or institutions are of any value to him who is defeated in battle; for all the good things of the conquered pass into the hands of the conquerors.

Considering the thousands of conflicts that have raged across the world since Plato's time, it would seem that war is an inevitable part of the human condition.

War not only remains an ever-present reality, it has also had undeniably crucial and far-reaching effects on human society and its development. As Keegan puts it, "History lessons remind us that the states in which we live . . . have come to us through conflict, often of the most bloodthirsty sort." Indeed, the world's first and oldest nation-state,

Egypt, was born out of a war between the two kingdoms that originally occupied the area; the modern nations of Europe rose from the wreckage of the sweeping barbarian invasions that destroyed the Roman Empire; and the United States was established by a bloody revolution between British colonists and their mother country.

Victory in these and other wars resulted from varying factors. Sometimes the side that possessed overwhelming numbers or the most persistence won; other times superior generalship and strategy played key roles. In many cases, the side with the most advanced and deadly weapons was victorious. In fact, the invention of increasingly lethal and devastating tools of war has largely driven the evolution of warfare, stimulating the development of new counter-weapons, strategies, and battlefield tactics. Among the major advances in ancient times were the composite bow, the war chariot, and the stone castle. Another was the Greek phalanx, a mass of close-packed spearmen marching forward as a unit, devastating all before it. In medieval times, the stirrup made it easier for a rider to stay on his horse, increasing the effectiveness of cavalry charges. And a progression of late medieval and modern weapons—including cannons, handguns, rifles, submarines, airplanes, missiles, and the atomic bomb—made warfare deadlier than ever.

Each such technical advance made war more devastating and therefore more feared. And to some degree, people are drawn to and fascinated by what they fear, which accounts for the high level of interest in studies of warfare and the weapons used to wage it. Military historian John Hackett writes:

An inevitable result of the convergence of two tendencies, fear of war and interest in the past, has seen a thirst for more information about the making of war in earlier times, not only in terms of tools, techniques, and methods used in warfare, but also of the people by whom wars are and have been fought and how men have set about the business of preparing for and fighting them.

These themes—the evolution of warfare and weapons and how it has affected various human societies—lie at the core of the books in Lucent's History of Weapons and Warfare series. Each book examines the warfare of a pivotal people or era in detail, exploring the beliefs about and motivations for war at the time, as well as specifics about weapons, strategies, battle formations, infantry, cavalry, sieges, naval tactics, and the lives and experiences of both military leaders and ordinary soldiers. Where possible, descriptions of actual campaigns and battles are provided to illustrate how these various factors came together and decided the fate of a city, a nation, or a people. Frequent quotations by contemporary participants or observers, as well as by noted modern military historians, add depth and authenticity. Each volume features an extensive annotated bibliography to guide those readers interested in further research to the most important and comprehensive works on warfare in the period in question. The series provides students and general readers with a useful means of understanding what is regrettably one of the driving forces of human history—violent human conflict.

Rome's Unique Approach to Warfare

As civilizations go, that of ancient Rome was unusually long-lived. From 753 B.C., the traditional date for the founding of the fledgling city, to A.D. 476, when the last western Roman emperor stepped down from his throne—never to be replaced—1,229 years elapsed. The Roman government and realm were at first ruled by kings. But in 509 B.C. the leading citizens dismantled the Monarchy and established a representative system—the Republic—controlled largely by the Senate. When the Republic fell in the late first century B.C., the first emperor, Augustus, took power; and his successors ruled for another five centuries.

War a Driving Force in Roman Affairs

Throughout all these centuries and changing political situations, war remained a driving and/or deciding force in Roman society and affairs. During the Monarchy and Republic, the Roman state almost continuously expanded its borders and influence through the force of arms; a series of bloody civil wars brought down the Republic; the early Empire expanded or maintained its borders through warfare; and in its last century, the realm underwent a contrasting shrinkage when the borders were threatened by invaders, whom the Roman military attempted but was unable to repel.

Not surprisingly, then, the Roman army was an ever-present institution that touched people on every level of society. Whether one served in it; commanded it; funded, fed, clothed, and housed it (a whopping 40 percent of the Empire's income went to maintaining it in the first century A.D.); suffered its wrath; or simply enjoyed its protection, one was affected by the military. And in a world where almost all nations had armies (as remains the case today), the Roman people accepted their own as necessary for their survival in a hostile world.

Historians and other students of Roman history study the Roman military for the many lessons such study can offer.

They try to determine how Rome waged war (i.e., the weapons, strategies, and tactics it used); to speculate on how military customs and methods were a reflection of Roman social and political ideals, as well as existing material resources and technology; and perhaps to learn something about human nature in the process.

The evidence clearly shows that military weapons, strategies, and tactics changed and evolved over the long centuries of Rome's existence, sometimes markedly so. For example, the Romans started out with a part-time citizen militia similar to that employed by ancient Greek cities; these early soldiers fought with thrusting spears in a rigid battlefield formation. Later, the Roman military instituted drastic changes, totally reorganizing their army; it became more flexible and emphasized the use of throwing spears and swords. The Romans also learned to build huge military camps to accommodate thousands of troops on the march and became masters of siege warfare. And when necessity dictated, some Roman soldiers became sailors who seized and maintained control of the Mediterranean seaways.

The Inspiration of Terror

As these and other aspects of Rome's military continued to develop and evolve, two realities of its overall approach to warfare remained more or less constant. First, Rome's military was (except at the very beginning and very end of its existence) extraordinarily well organized, well disciplined, and efficient. These factors certainly contributed to its reputation as a force to be feared. But even more telling was its often systematic, naked, and merciless brutality when on the

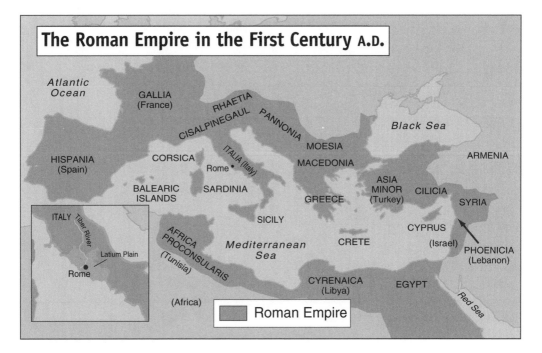

The Roman Empire in the First Century A.D.

offensive. In a memorable passage, the second-century B.C. Greek historian Polybius, who wrote extensively about the Roman army, recalled an assault on an enemy town in Spain. When the Roman commander felt enough of his men had entered the town, he

> let loose the majority of them against the inhabitants, according to the Roman custom; their orders were to exterminate every form of life they encountered, sparing none, but not to start pillaging until the word was given to do so. This practice is adopted to inspire terror, and so when cities are taken by the Romans you may often see not only the corpses of human beings, but dogs cut in half and the dismembered limbs of other animals, and on this occasion the carnage was especially frightful because of the large size of the population.[1]

Many other examples of Roman use of extreme violence to instill terror can be cited. To name only a few: condemning deserters to be eaten by half-starved beasts or trampled by elephants; beheading all the leaders of a rebellious town and selling the rest of the population into slavery; and worse, completely obliterating two enemy cities—Corinth and Carthage—in the same year (146 B.C.) as an object lesson to others who might contemplate opposing Rome.

The Roman army could be merciless and brutal when commanders felt the situation warranted it. This engraving shows Roman soldiers devastating an enemy town.

Leniency for the Defeated

Such brutality in wartime, by itself, was not unique to the Romans. History is in fact replete with others who did so, from the Assyrians in the early first millennium B.C., to the Huns in the fourth century A.D., to the Japanese in World War II. What made the Romans quite different than the others was how they usually followed up their victories. In short, the Romans possessed a gift, perhaps even a genius, for political conciliation and organization. With rare exceptions, once Rome had won a war, it was lenient with its former enemies. More often, Roman leaders opted for the wiser and more fruitful approach of making treaties with the defeated and granting them Roman citizenship and legal privileges. They also initiated the habit of introducing the Latin language, as well as Roman ideas, laws, and customs, to non-Latin peoples, in a sense "Romanizing" them. "What made the Romans so remarkable," comments noted classical scholar Michael Grant, was the combination of their cruelty during wartime

with a talent for patient political reasonableness that was unique in the ancient world. . . . On the whole, Rome found it advisable, and was encouraged by its religion, to keep its bargains with its allies, displaying a self-restraint, a readiness to compromise, and a calculated generosity that the world had never seen. And so the allies, too, had little temptation to feel misused.[2]

This powerful combination of strength and conciliation served Rome well and made its long life possible. As long as Roman armies were able to win most of the wars they entered and afterward make constructive alliances with the defeated, the Roman state survived. When, in the fourth and fifth centuries, this process weakened and finally broke down (thanks to the decline of both the army and the quality of the political leadership), the old Roman world was doomed.

CHAPTER ONE

The Early Roman Army

The nature and details of Rome's first military efforts are lost in the mists of time, as are the exact origins of the Romans themselves. Regarding the latter, perhaps about 1000 B.C. tribal peoples calling themselves Latins moved into the fertile plain of Latium, situated in west-central Italy between the Mediterranean Sea and the rugged Apennine Mountains. Primitive farmers, some of them estab-

Rome began as and always remained mainly an agricultural society. The stone-lined well in the foreground and nearby stone huts were typical sights on Roman farms and country estates.

THE INFLUENTIAL ETRUSCANS

The Etruscans, who inhabited Etruria (the region lying north of Rome) during the Monarchy and early Republic, fought the Romans at intervals over a span of several centuries. All the while, especially at times when relations between the two peoples were cordial, the inhabitants of Rome felt the cultural influence of these more culturally advanced neighbors. The Etruscans were an energetic, talented, highly civilized people who lived in well-fortified cities often featuring paved streets laid out in logical, convenient grid patterns. Most of what is known about them comes from excavations of their tombs, which began in earnest in the nineteenth century. In one area alone—Tarquinii (a few miles northwest of Rome)—archaeologists found over five thousand Etruscan tombs in the 1960s. Many of those explored have revealed beautiful wall paintings, sculptures, weapons, pottery, and other grave goods, all providing evidence of a culture that both impressed and inspired the Romans.

lished villages on seven low hills near a bend in the Tiber River; and in time, probably in the eighth or seventh century B.C., these villages came together to form the city of Rome.

More accurately, early Rome was a small city-state, composed of a modest urban center (with dirt roads and buildings made of wood and thatch) surrounded by a few dozen (eventually a few hundred) square miles of farmland and some rural villages. War and peace, as well as other crucial decisions of government, were the province of the local kings; although they increasingly came to listen and respond to the demands of a small group of well-to-do landowners—the patricians—who met in the Senate, at first an advisory board to the Monarchy.

When a Roman king and his advisers decided to go to war, they did not have a class of full-time professional soldiers to draw on, as became the case much later in Rome's history. The writings of later ancient historians suggest that the earliest Roman army was a militia. Like the colonial militiamen who fought the British during the American Revolution, the Roman militia consisted of a group of nonprofessionals called into service during an emergency or when otherwise needed and then disbanded after a short campaign.

As might be expected, the early Roman army was under the direct command of the king; but as it grew larger, he needed officers to help him control it. The first such unit commanders were three tribunes. The Latin word *tribunus* means "tribal officer," and each tribune appropriately commanded 1,000 men, all landowners, from one of Rome's three traditional native tribes. The total force of 3,000 infantrymen (foot soldiers) was called a legion (from the word *legio*, meaning "the levying"). Each of the various subdivisions of a tribe supplied 100 men, a basic unit that became known as a century. The legion was supported by about 300 cavalry (horse soldiers), drawn from

During the early years of the Republic, Roman soldiers resembled this Greek-style hoplite, who relied on his spear and shield.

the ranks of a well-to-do social class known as the *equites*, or "knights," among the few who could afford to keep horses.

Armor and Weapons

The exact way these part-time soldiers fought is uncertain. But by the early sixth century B.C. at the latest, they had adopted many of the same fighting methods practiced by the Greek cities that had grown up in southern Italy in the eighth and seventh centuries B.C.; and also from the Etruscans, the people who inhabited Etruria, the region directly north of

Rome. (The Etruscans had themselves already adopted Greek military methods.) In copying the Greek military system, the early Romans demonstrated one of their hallmarks, which was apparently well established by that time. This was a strong sense of practicality coupled with their talent for imitating others, an ability to borrow the best attributes of foreign cultures and to adapt these to their own special needs.

The Greek system the Romans both adopted and adapted was built around hoplites—armored infantry soldiers. Evidence shows that these soldiers wore cuirasses (breastplates), helmets, and greaves (lower-leg protectors) fashioned of beaten bronze, an alloy of copper and tin. Many of the earliest Roman hoplite helmets were Villanovan in style—shaped like a deep bowl turned upside down and sporting a tall, pointed metal crest at the

EARLY ROMAN HELMETS

The helmets worn by the first Roman soldiers, like those of the neighboring Etruscans and other early Italian groups, were Villanovan style (named after an early Italian people). To date, the remains of about thirty such helmets have been discovered in Italy. As military historian Peter Connolly explains in this excerpt from Greece and Rome at War:

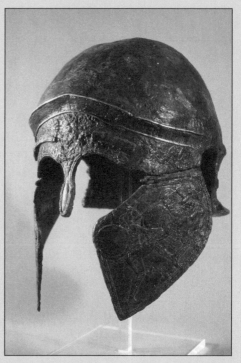

More than half of these are of the metal crested type. This was an exaggerated form of a central European type. It was made in two pieces joined along the edge of the crest. This was done by making one half slightly larger than the other and folding the surplus metal over the smaller half to hold it in position. The lower edges of the cap at the front and the back also overlapped and were riveted together. The joint was reinforced by two rectangular plates which were riveted on. These helmets, like all other armor of the period, were decorated with bosses [small studs or other raised ornaments]. . . . Most of these helmets and the later Roman helmets are considerably oversize and it seems very likely that they all had a thick padded undercap, probably made of felt.

In addition to Villanovan helmets, some early Roman soldiers wore the Chalcidian style, shown here.

top. (The Villanovans were an Italian culture who predated and influenced the Etruscans in the region north of Rome.) As time went on, other types of helmet became common, among them the Greek Chalcidian style, with wide cheek pieces and a thin strip covering the nose; and the Negau type (named after a village in what is now Yugoslavia, where archaeologists discovered several specimens), which was conical in shape and often topped by a crest made of horsehair.

Also for defense, the early Roman hoplite carried a round shield made of wood or wicker covered by either several layers of ox hide or, for those soldiers who could afford it, a layer of bronze. About three feet in diameter, it had a single central handgrip, which made holding the shield in the upright defensive position for longer than a few minutes quite difficult. Some evidence suggests that the Romans eventually adopted a distinctive and much more efficient gripping system pio-

The remains of Greek bronze sword blades illustrate only part of the wide range of sizes and types used by early Mediterranean hoplites, including Roman ones.

This excellent modern illustration shows some of the armor and weapons typical of central Italy in the sixth century B.C., including bronze greaves and both round and oblong shields. The man in the middle wears a "pot" helmet, which was common at that time.

neered by the Greeks. In the center of the inside of the shield was a bronze strip with a loop, through which the hoplite passed his left forearm; and on the rim was a leather handle, which he grasped with his left hand. Because this system allowed the shield to rest on the hoplite's arm, it helped to relieve the burden of the shield's considerable weight; also, if need be, he could let go of the handle and hold a spare weapon in his left hand without losing his shield.

The Roman hoplite's main weapon was a thrusting spear, which he jabbed overhand at an enemy soldier. He also carried

a sword, usually of bronze but occasionally of iron, which he used if he lost or broke his spear. Some of the early Roman swords had long blades suitable for slashing and hacking, while others bore shorter, pointed blades effective for stabbing and poking.

A full array of such armor and weapons was very expensive. The ores containing the metals had to be mined and transported; and separating the metals from the ores, as well as shaping the separated metals, was laborious and required specially trained workers. "All the bronze weapons were cast from molten [melted] metal," says noted military historian Peter Connolly. "Iron weapons had to be beaten into shape as it was impossible to obtain sufficient temperature for the casting of iron. In fact, beaten weapons were far stronger than cast ones."[3] Because the hoplite's armor and weapons were so expensive, most, if not all, Roman hoplites were members of the well-to-do classes.

The rest of the troops, who accompanied and supported the core group of hoplites, were poorer folk whose costumes and weapons varied according to their individual circumstances. Most wore no armor, although some probably had metal helmets. For defense, many apparently carried an oval or oblong wooden shield one or two feet longer than a hoplite's, with a small copper or bronze plate attached to the front. This was the direct ancestor of the *scutum*, the rectangular version wielded by later Roman legionaries. The weapons carried by these early support troops included spears, javelins (throwing spears), swords, daggers, axes, and, in the case of the poorest of the lot, probably sickles and other farm implements.

The Roman Phalanx

It is not completely clear how early Roman commanders organized and utilized their hoplites and support troops. But it was likely at least similar to the way the Greeks organized and utilized these units. Greek hoplites stood in ranks (lines), one behind the other, creating a formidable battlefield formation called a phalanx. A depth of eight ranks was most common. But on occasion there might be considerably more than eight or as few as three or four ranks. In forming the phalanx, they created a veritable wall of upright shields and forward-pointing spears; and when they marched

The Roman Phalanx

Open Phalanx
5–6 feet between soldiers

Closed Phalanx
When maneuvering into battle the rear half of each file moves forward to create a "shield wall" with 2–3 feet between soldiers.

forward, the formation was extremely difficult to stop or defend against.

The ranks of hoplites within the phalanx were tightly organized into various divisions and units for maximum fighting efficiency. Such organization varied somewhat from one place to another, as city-states in Greece, Italy, and elsewhere attempted to meet their own needs. But scholars believe that all Greek and other Mediterranean phalanxes based on them, including that of the Romans, evolved from a basic prototype that developed in the early first millennium B.C. It probably consisted of units of a hundred men, each called a *lochos*. (The Roman version of the *lochos* was the hundred-man century.) This so-called "archaic *lochos*" may have broken down into smaller units of fifty and twenty-five men. Later, various city-states, including Rome, developed their own subdivisions for the formation; unfortunately, the exact size and look of the Roman versions are unknown.

Whatever its local variations, the traditional phalanx employed by the Greeks, Etruscans, Romans, and others was an extremely effective offensive unit in its heyday (ca. 700–350 B.C.) for two reasons. First, it afforded its members a high degree of protection. When assembled in open order, they stood about five to six feet apart; but in close order—perhaps two to three feet apart, the mode most often adopted when closing with an enemy—their uplifted shields created a formidable unbroken protective barrier. Each shield protected its owner's left side, but also the right side and spear arm of the man standing on his left. "If the formation

broke," historian John Warry explains, "this advantage was lost; the army which broke an enemy formation while preserving its own had won a battle. Once its own formation had been broken, an army usually took to flight."[4]

Defeated hoplites who did choose to make a run for it knew they could not make it far burdened by their heavy armor. And the shield was usually the first item to be discarded. Famous across the ancient Mediterranean world was a poem by a seventh-century B.C. Greek, Archilochus: "Well, what if some barbaric Thracian glories in the perfect shield I left under a bush? I was sorry to leave it—but I saved my skin. Does it matter? O hell, I'll buy a better one!"[5]

The other factor that made the phalanx so formidable was its tremendous and lethal forward momentum. As the formation made contact with the enemy lines, the hoplites in the front rank jabbed their spears at their opponents, usually aiming for the belly, groin, or legs; at the same time, the hoplites in the rear ranks pushed at their comrades' backs, pressing them forward at the enemy.

Meanwhile, there were various standard pre-, mid-, and postbattle practices undertaken by Greek and presumably Etruscan, Roman, and other Italian hoplites. As they occurred in fairly rapid succession, these included: sacrificing a goat or other animal just prior to battle to determine if the religious signs were favorable; listening to a spirit-raising speech by the commanding general; singing a battle hymn (paean) to steel their nerves and intimidate the enemy; breaking into a running charge when nearing the enemy line;

ROME'S FIRST CONQUEST

According to Roman legend, most of those who initially settled in Rome were men who had difficulty obtaining brides. To solve this problem, the founder, Romulus, came up with an audacious plan. He invited the residents of a number of neighboring towns, all inhabited by a Latin people called the Sabines, to a great religious festival where athletic games and theatrical performances would be staged. His real intention, however, was not to foster friendship, but rather to steal the Sabine women. "On the appointed day," Livy wrote in his famous history of Rome, "crowds flocked to Rome. . . . All the Sabines were there . . . with their wives and children. . . . Then the great moment came. . . . At a given signal, all the able-bodied [Roman] men burst through the crowd and seized the young women."

Romulus assured the captured brides that they would be well treated and tried to talk them into accepting their new situation. Soon, however, the male Sabines attacked Rome in an effort to win back their women. Soldiers from the Sabine city of Cures, led by their king, Titus Tatius, managed to surround Rome, and there ensued a great battle in which many on both sides were killed. Suddenly, the former Sabine women rushed out and demanded a truce. They could not simply stand by, they declared, and watch their fathers, brothers, and husbands slaughter one another. The result was a treaty in which the two sides agreed to merge as one people, with Romulus and Titus Tatius as joint rulers. Rome had made its first conquest and absorption of neighboring people, opening the way for the newly founded city's spectacular rise to greatness.

screaming the war cry during the charge; and if they were victorious, erecting on the battlefield a trophy, a wooden framework displaying captured enemy arms, to give thanks to the gods.

The lightly armored and unarmored soldiers (skirmishers) and cavalrymen who supported the Roman hoplites took part in most of these same activities. The nature of the support they provided during actual battle would have depended on the individual situation. If the phalanx was opposed by another phalanx, the skirmishers fended off the enemy's own skirmishers, who otherwise would try to break up the Roman phalanx by attacking its sides and rear. If, on the other hand,

the enemy army was composed of a mass of lightly armored or unarmored troops rather than hoplites, the Roman skirmishers likely chased down and killed or captured the enemy soldiers after the phalanx had defeated them. These early Roman skirmishers probably played a more direct and independent role in hilly terrain; there, they could move faster and maneuver more easily than the heavily armored hoplites. (And in any case, the phalanx itself needed relatively flat ground with few obstacles to operate efficiently.) The early Roman cavalry also provided support by protecting the flanks of the phalanx and chasing down fleeing enemies. Because stirrups and saddles had not yet been invented, riders had difficulty staying on swiftly moving horses, so cavalry could not be used for direct charges on infantry, as it was in later ages.

The Servian Reform and Roman Republic

Eventually the Roman military, with its elite phalanx and mass of lighter-armed support troops, underwent a major reorganization. Later ancient writers, including the great first-century B.C. Roman historian Livy, claimed the reorganization took place in the middle of the sixth century B.C.; and it is usually referred to as the Servian reform after Servius Tullius, the legendary sixth king of Rome, who supposedly ordered it. Mod-

ern scholars believe that this military reform occurred somewhat later, however, and perhaps over a more extended period.

Whatever the correct dating of the event, Livy explained that the government instituted a census of the male population and divided it, along with the army itself, into six classes according to degrees of wealth. About the wealthiest group, he wrote:

> Of those whose property was rated at a capital value of 100,000 *asses* or more [an *as* being a common unit of Roman currency], 80 centuries were formed, 40 of "seniors" and 40 of "juniors." This whole group was

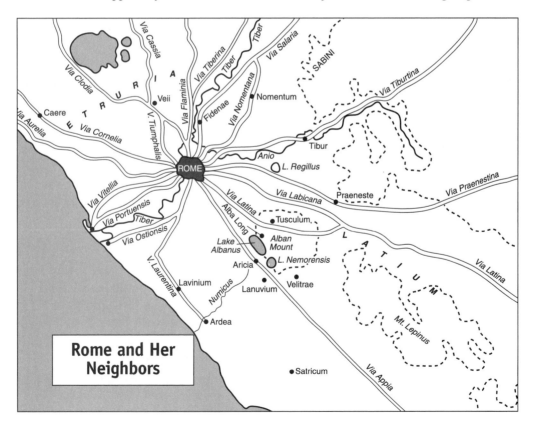

Rome and Her Neighbors

known as the First Class. The seniors were for civil defense, the juniors for service in the field. All were required to equip themselves with helmet, round shield, greaves, and breastplate. The defensive armor was of bronze. Their weapons of offense were the sword and spear.[6]

The armor and weapons Livy describes here make it clear that the members of the First Class manned the phalanx. Or more precisely, half of them did. The "seniors," probably men over the age of forty-five or perhaps fifty, were assigned to "civil defense," meaning guarding Rome's urban center in an emergency; that left forty centuries of younger men—a total of four thousand—to fight as hoplites in the phalanx. The second, third, fourth, and fifth classes were made up of progressively lighter-armed troops whose task was to support the phalanx on the battlefield; and the sixth class, whose members were the poorest of Rome's citizens, was exempt from military service.

The Servian reform may have roughly coincided with a political revolution just as crucial to Rome's future. Having grown tired of rule by kings, in about 509 B.C. the patricians dismantled the Monarchy and in its place installed the Republic, a government based on the more democratic idea of rule by representatives of the people. However, Roman leaders at first defined "the people" rather narrowly. Only free adult males who owned weapons (and were therefore eligible for military service), a group that made up a minority of the population,

could vote or hold public office. Some of these citizens met periodically in an assembly that proposed and voted on new laws and also annually elected two consuls (administrator-generals) to run the state and lead the army. The other legislative body, the Senate, was composed exclusively of well-to-do patricians, who held their positions for life. The senators usually dictated the policies of the consuls and, through the use of wealth and high position, indirectly influenced the way the members of the assembly voted. So the Senate held the real power in Rome, making the Republic an oligarchy (a government headed by an elite few) rather than a true democracy.

Warfare an Instrument of Expansion

In the Republic's first century, Rome began the physical expansion that would eventually lead it to Mediterranean mastery. And its land army, now commanded by the two consuls (and below them the traditional tribunes), was the principal instrument of that expansion. (Still strictly a land power, Rome had no navy at this time.) At first, the Romans' enemies—other Italian tribal peoples—were situated nearby. As military historian Lawrence Keppie points out, in these years

> the wars between Rome and her neighbors were little more than scuffles between armed raiding bands of a few hundred [or thousand] men at most. . . . Fidenae, against which the Romans were fighting in 499 [B.C.], now lies within the motorway circuit round

24

Etruscan elders scatter in fear as Roman troops capture the important Etruscan citadel of Veii in 396 B.C. Eventually Rome defeated and absorbed all the Etruscan cities.

modern Rome, and is all but swallowed up in its northern suburbs.[7]

Over time, however, the Roman army pushed the borders of Rome's territory and influence ever outward. After absorbing the villages and farmlands of the Latium plain, Rome fought a ten-year-long war against the Etruscans, capturing the important Etruscan city of Veii in 396 B.C. By this time, the army had expanded to a legion/phalanx of six thousand men, supported by several thousand light-armed troops and some eighteen hundred cavalry. Because the legionaries had to spend more and more

time away from home, the state began to pay them a daily cash allowance for the days they served. (They were still part-time militiamen rather than full-time professionals, however; in this period the average soldier probably served for no more than a few weeks or months at a stretch on two or three occasions in his lifetime.)

This expanded version of the early Roman army met its greatest test yet in 390 B.C. A large force of tribal Gauls, who had earlier crossed the Alps into northern Italy, descended through Etruria and marched on Rome. The Roman phalanx assembled near the Allia River (a few

An old woodcut depicts the Roman defeat at the Allia River in 390 B.C. The disaster prompted a number of significant military reforms that made the Roman army much more effective.

miles north of the city), expecting to easily repulse the invaders. But though the Gallic army lacked organization and discipline, its fearsome-looking warriors—nearly naked, longhaired, and wearing war paint—staged a wild, screaming charge that completely terrified the unprepared Roman soldiers. According to Livy:

> In the lines of the legionaries—officers and men alike—there was no trace of the old Roman manhood. They fled in panic, so blinded by everything but saving their skins that, in spite of the fact that the Tiber

lay in their way, most of them tried to get to Veii, once an enemy town, instead of making for their own homes in Rome. . . . The main body of the army, at the first sound of the Gallic war-cry . . . hardly waited even to see their strange enemy from the ends of the earth; they made no attempt at resistance . . . but fled before they had lost a single man. None fell fighting; they were cut down from behind as they struggled to force a way to safety through the heaving mass of their fellow-fugitives. Near the bank of the river there was a terrible slaughter; the whole left wing of the army had gone that way and had flung away their arms [i.e., their hoplite armor and weapons] in the desperate hope of getting over. Many could not swim and many others in their exhausted state were dragged under water by the weight of their equipment and drowned. . . . The Gauls could hardly believe their eyes, so easy, so miraculously swift their victory had been.[8]

After the Roman defeat, the Gauls proceeded to sack Rome. They eventually withdrew, but only after demanding and getting a large ransom of gold. The anniversary of the humiliating defeat, July 18, thereafter became known in Rome as the dark "Day of Allia," an unlucky date on the calendar. More important to Rome's future, the event convinced Roman leaders that the traditional military system, including its training and deployment of soldiers, was inadequate. They took the bold step of instituting radically new battle formations and tactics. In the fullness of time, this move turned out to have enormous consequences for Rome and ultimately for all the peoples of the Mediterranean world.

CHAPTER TWO

The Development of Manipular Tactics

In an effort to avoid any further disasters like the humiliating defeat at Allia, the Romans decided to institute radical military reforms. Under a strong leader named Marcus Furius Camillus, who went on to defeat the Gauls, Rome abandoned the rigid, sometimes inflexible phalanx. In the coming years, Camillus and other reformers created an army in which a legion broke down into several smaller units on the battlefield. These units, called maniples (*manipuli*, meaning "handfuls") were each capable of independent action and could be combined or separated at will, making the whole army much more flexible. Moreover, the Romans discarded the circular hoplite shield and adopted the more protective oval (later rectangular) *scutum;* they also largely replaced the thrusting spear with a shorter throwing spear, the *pilum.* About this revolutionary new "manipular" system, Lawrence Keppie writes:

> The new flexibility of battle-order and equipment were cardinal factors in the Romans' eventual conquest of the Mediterranean world. The hoplites had worked in close order at short range, but the new legionaries were mostly equipped to engage with the *pilum* at long range, then to charge forward into already disorganized enemy ranks, before setting to [getting to work] with sword and shield.[9]

Specific Soldiers with Specific Jobs

As Keppie emphasizes, the manipular system's high degree of flexibility was the key factor in the spectacular military successes the Roman Republic achieved in the centuries that followed. Once it was fully developed and tested, a process that may have taken several decades or perhaps a century or more, the new system was unlike any other in the known world. It was logically and strictly organized; it fully exploited the strengths of various kinds of fighters, who were all well trained and well drilled in battle tactics; and it allowed for methodical, well-ordered reactions to various contingencies that might occur on the battlefield, including the need for strategic retreat.

To understand the components and tactics of the manipular system, one should first imagine a Roman army assembled on the battlefield, facing and ready to engage an enemy force. In Polybius's time (the second century B.C.), the front of such a Roman army consisted of a long line, a few ranks deep, of light-armed skirmishers. These were the *velites*, very young men usually wearing no armor and carrying throwing spears. According to Polybius, "They also wear a plain helmet which is sometimes covered with a piece of wolf's skin or some-

thing similar, which serves both to protect and identify the soldier."[10]

Arrayed behind the *velites* was the bulk of the army, with the infantry deployed in manipular fashion, that is, with the maniples assembled in three long lines, one behind the other, facing the enemy. In each line there were spaces separating the maniples, each space being the same width as a maniple. At the same time, the maniples and spaces of the three lines were staggered in such a way that there was open space in front and back of each maniple, overall rendering a sort of checkerboard effect. (Because this pattern resembled the dots representing the number five on dice cubes, which the Romans called a *quincunx*, they gave the battlefield formation the same name.)

The main factor that made each of the three lines of maniples distinct was that it

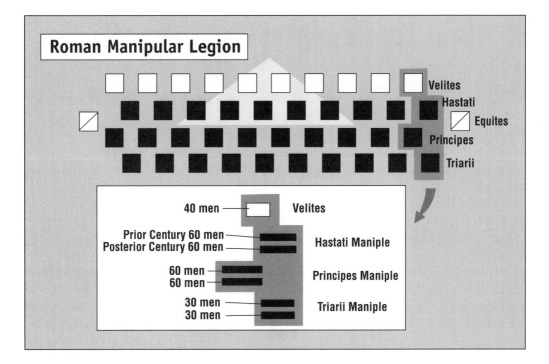

Roman Manipular Legion

Velites
Hastati
Equites
Principes
Triarii

40 men — Velites
Prior Century 60 men — Hastati Maniple
Posterior Century 60 men —
60 men — Principes Maniple
60 men —
30 men — Triarii Maniple
30 men —

In these reconstructions of early Roman legionaries, the hastatus *at left bears a* scutum *and two* pila. *The man at right is a* veles, *a skirmisher armed with javelins.*

contained a specific kind of soldier with a specific job to do. The front line was made up of the *hastati*, young men with a minimum of experience but possessing a great deal of vigor and endurance. Each maniple of *hastati* (and each maniple in the other two lines) was composed of two centuries, one positioned behind the other. (By this time a century contained 80 rather than 100 men.) The front century in a maniple was termed the "prior" and the

back one the "posterior." Each maniple of *hastati* had 60 men to a century and therefore 120 men in all. (The other 20 of each century's standard 80 men were *velites*, who stood in their separate line.)

Behind the *hastati* were the *principes*, experienced fighters in the prime of life (probably aged twenty-five to thirty). Their maniples were also composed of 120 men each. Both the *hastati* and *principes* wore full armor, consisting of cuirass, helmet, and greaves, and each was armed with two *pila* (one light, the other heavy) and a double-edged thrusting sword (the *gladius*, which had originated in Spain).

Finally, the rear line was made up of the *triarii*, older veterans who lacked the physical endurance of the others but possessed more experience. Each century of *triarii* had 30 men, so these rear maniples had 60 rather than 120 men each. Polybius says that the *triarii* had the same armor and weapons as the others, "except that instead of the throwing-spear, the *triarii* carry long thrusting spears."[11]

Executing the Manipular Tactic

The manner in which these specialized kinds of troops fought was as follows. After the Roman commander signaled his trumpeter to sound the attack, the army advanced on the enemy. When the enemy line drew close enough, the *velites*, still in the forefront of the Roman forces, opened the battle by charging forward and hurling their javelins. "The purpose of this," Peter Connolly explains, "was to try to break up the enemy formation in anticipation of the charge of the [Roman] heavy infantry. . . . When both sides had lightly armed troops in front, this tactic was neutralized."[12]

As the two armies neared each other, another trumpet blast signaled for the most common Roman battlefield maneuver of republican times—the manipular tactic—to begin. The *velites* suddenly retreated, passing quickly through the open spaces in the three lines of maniples and re-forming their line in the rear,

behind the *triarii*. Meanwhile, after the last of the skirmishers had made it past the *hastati* in the front line, the posterior centuries of *hastati* swiftly moved from behind the prior centuries and filled the gaps in the line. This formidable solid bank of infantry now charged forward, the men shouting fiercely in unison in an attempt to frighten the enemy. At a distance of about a hundred feet, the *hastati* hurled their light javelins and a few seconds later followed with their heavy ones. Then they drew their swords, rushed forward, and crashed into the enemy ranks with as much impact as possible.

The charge of the *hastati* sometimes damaged and demoralized the enemy enough to force his retreat, giving the Romans an easy victory. On the other hand, if after a while the *hastati* could make no headway or appeared to be in trouble, the Roman trumpet signaled the next stage of the manipular tactic. The *hastati* retreated, their posterior centuries returning to their original positions behind the prior centuries. They then hurried through the gaps separating the maniples of *principes* and *triarii* and stood behind the *triarii*. Meanwhile, just as the *hastati* had done earlier, the *principes* formed a solid line and charged the enemy, who now had to face a force of fresh soldiers with even more battle experience than the *hastati*.

If the charge of the *principes* was not enough to defeat the enemy, they retreated the same way the *hastati* had and filled the gaps between the *hastati*'s maniples. Then one of two scenarios played out. If it looked as though the battle could still be

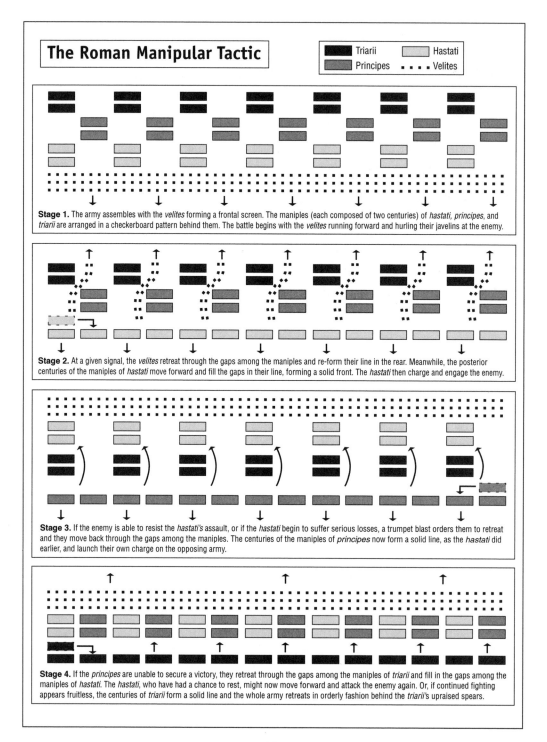

The Roman Manipular Tactic

Triarii — Hastati
Principes · · · · Velites

Stage 1. The army assembles with the *velites* forming a frontal screen. The maniples (each composed of two centuries) of *hastati, principes*, and *triarii* are arranged in a checkerboard pattern behind them. The battle begins with the *velites* running forward and hurling their javelins at the enemy.

Stage 2. At a given signal, the *velites* retreat through the gaps among the maniples and re-form their line in the rear. Meanwhile, the posterior centuries of the maniples of *hastati* move forward and fill the gaps in their line, forming a solid front. The *hastati* then charge and engage the enemy.

Stage 3. If the enemy is able to resist the *hastati's* assault, or if the *hastati* begin to suffer serious losses, a trumpet blast orders them to retreat and they move back through the gaps among the maniples. The centuries of the maniples of *principes* now form a solid line, as the *hastati* did earlier, and launch their own charge on the opposing army.

Stage 4. If the *principes* are unable to secure a victory, they retreat through the gaps among the maniples of *triarii* and fill in the gaps among the maniples of *hastati*. The *hastati*, who have had a chance to rest, might now move forward and attack the enemy again. Or, if continued fighting appears fruitless, the centuries of *triarii* form a solid line and the whole army retreats in orderly fashion behind the *triarii's* upraised spears.

won, the *hastati*, having had a chance to rest, pressed forward and had a second go at the enemy. However, if the Roman commander decided it was best to quit and fight again another day, he ordered the fresh and very experienced *triarii* to enter the fray. They formed a solid line and pointed their spears forward, in phalanx fashion, creating a protective barrier behind which the whole army retreated in an orderly manner.

Other Military Developments

Coinciding with the development of manipular tactics, the Romans instituted other organizational changes that made their army more effective and formidable. By the 360s B.C., about three decades after the Allia debacle, the Roman military consisted of two full legions, each with about 4,200 to 5,000 men, all Roman citizens. And by 311 there were four legions of citizens, which thereafter became the standard minimum. Each consul usually commanded two such legions. In addition, when campaigning, a consul's two citizen legions were accompanied and supported by two more legions drawn from Rome's allies (Italian peoples it had conquered and signed treaties with). These noncitizen soldiers were collectively referred to as the *alae sociorum* ("wings of allies").

No other Italian peoples possessed armies of such size, effective organization, and fighting caliber. So it is not surprising that the newly refurbished Roman army swiftly won control of all Italy. By 290 B.C. the Romans had conquered the fierce Samnites and other hill tribes of central Italy; and by 265 the Greek cities scattered across the peninsula's southern sector had been absorbed into the Roman sphere. Rome next set its sights on several prosperous islands and coastlines lying beyond the shores of Italy. The powerful trading city and empire of Carthage, centered at the northern tip of Tunisia, on the African coast, fell to Roman steel after the three devastating Punic Wars, fought between 264 and 146 B.C.

An Ability to Sustain Huge Losses

Rome's impressive victories in these wars were not solely the result of the army's excellent organization, discipline, training, and weapons. As a people, the Romans possessed an astonishing, dogged determination and will to survive, a never-say-die attitude that allowed them on repeated occasions to sustain huge losses and still bounce back and defeat the enemy. In fact, despite their extraordinary organization, Roman manipular armies did sometimes suffer defeats. The classic example—the Battle of Cannae—showed clearly that while Roman battle tactics were potentially very flexible, their ultimate effectiveness depended in large degree on the quality of the commanders who executed them; and even if said leaders were competent, their talents and efforts might be blunted or even nullified if the enemy commander was gifted enough.

The enemy commander at Cannae was Hannibal of Carthage (247–182 B.C.), unarguably one of the finest military generals in history. During the early stages of the Second Punic War, the largest and bloodiest conflict fought on earth up to that time, he defeated one Roman army after another, inflicting horrendous losses and bringing Rome almost to its knees.

SAMNITE WARS

Among the toughest enemies early Roman armies faced were the Samnites, a sturdy, often warlike people who inhabited the valleys of the central and southern Apennines. In the middle of the fourth century B.C., Samnite territory and population were probably twice as big as those of Rome and the largest of any single Italian people. Rome fought three wars with the Samnites. The first one (343–341 B.C.) arose when the Samnites attacked Capua (in Campania, south of Rome) and the town asked the Romans for assistance. At one point, the Roman army mutinied because it felt it was fighting too far from home. However, the war ended with Rome in control of northern Campania. The Second Samnite War (326–304 B.C.) resulted when the Samnites again intruded into Campania, this time occupying the town of Neapolis (modern Naples). The Romans drove the Samnite garrison out, but in 321 B.C. the enemy trapped a Roman army at the Caudine Forks (near Capua), forcing the Roman troops to surrender, a humiliation the Romans never forgot. Still, the Romans rebounded and eventually defeated the Samnites, who had to vacate Campania for good. In the Third Samnite War (298–290 B.C.), the Romans carried the fighting directly into Samnite territory. Despite a courageous defense put up by the local towns, the Romans ravaged one Samnite valley after another until the enemy had no choice but to surrender. Rome absorbed a good deal of Samnite territory and forced the Samnites to become Roman allies, thereby removing the greatest single obstacle in the path of Rome's conquest of the Italian peninsula.

The Samnites force the Romans to pass under a yoke, a sign of submission, at the Caudine Forks.

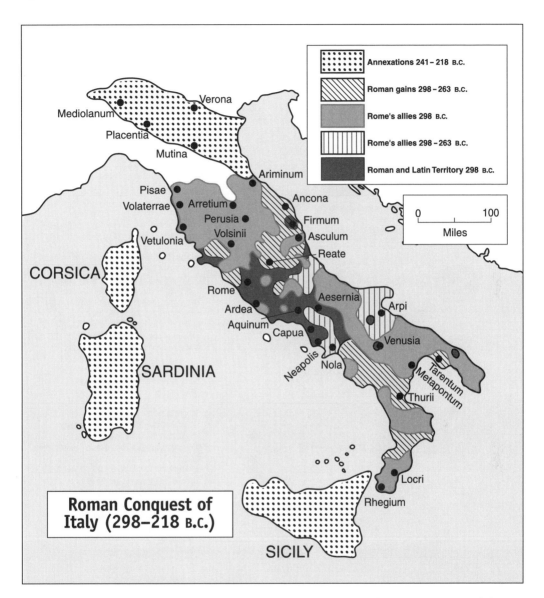

	Annexations 241–218 B.C.
	Roman gains 298–263 B.C.
	Rome's allies 298 B.C.
	Rome's allies 298–263 B.C.
	Roman and Latin Territory 298 B.C.

0   100
Miles

Verona
Mediolanum
Placentia
Mutina
Ariminum
Pisae
Volaterrae   Arretium   Ancona
Perusia   Firmum
Volsinii   Asculum
Vetulonia   Reate
CORSICA
Rome
Aesernia   Arpi
Ardea
Aquinum   Capua   Venusia
SARDINIA   Neapolis   Nola   Tarentum
Metapontum
Thurii
Locri
Rhegium
**Roman Conquest of
Italy (298–218 B.C.)**
SICILY

Hannibal's greatest victory, and Rome's darkest hour, came in 216 B.C. A huge Roman army of some 75,000 to 80,000 men, commanded by the consuls Paullus and Varro, confronted Hannibal's 40,000 troops on a small plain near the village of Cannae, in southeastern Italy. Because the plain was very narrow, the Romans made their maniples narrower and deeper than usual.

Seeing that the Romans had assembled for battle in their usual manner, with the infantry maniples massed in the center, Hannibal anticipated that they would attempt to attack and overwhelm his own center. So he set a trap for them. Instead of placing his

Battle of Cannae

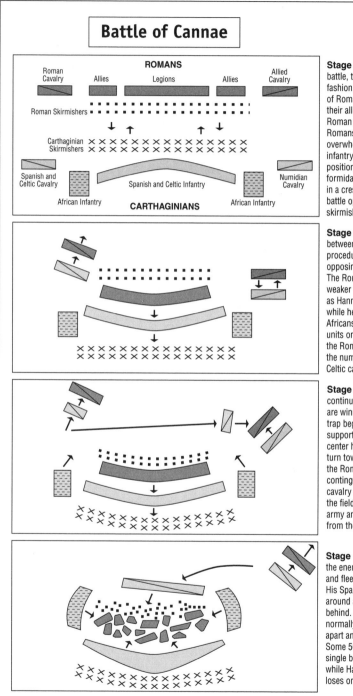

Stage 1. As the opposing armies prepare for battle, the Romans form ranks in their usual fashion, with their strongest infantry—made up of Roman legionaries—in the center, flanked by their allied infantry, and on the wings the Roman and allied cavalry units. Aware that the Romans mean to aim for his own center and overwhelm it, Hannibal moves his strongest infantry—the Africans—back to holding positions on the flanks and draws up his less formidable Spanish and Celtic infantry units in a crescent formation in the center. The battle opens with a clash of the light-armed skirmishers of the opposing sides.

Stage 2. After the initial, indecisive exchange between the skirmishers, per the usual procedure they retreat to the rear and the opposing infantry units advance on each other. The Roman legions and allied units push the weaker Carthaginian center backward, just as Hannibal had anticipated they would, while he shrewdly continues to hold his Africans in reserve. Meanwhile, the cavalry units on the right clash, while on the left the Roman cavalry breaks and flees from the numerically superior Spanish and Celtic cavalry.

Stage 3. As the Roman infantrymen continue to press forward, believing they are winning the battle, Hannibal's brilliant trap begins to spring on them. With the added support of his skirmishers in the rear, his center holds. At the same time, his Africans turn toward the center and begin to envelop the Roman flanks. Meanwhile, as a small contingent of his Spanish and Celtic cavalry pursues the Roman horsemen off the field, the rest swing behind the Roman army and attack the Roman allied cavalry from the rear.

Stage 4. Assaulted front and back by the enemy, the Roman allied cavalry breaks and flees, pursued by Hannibal's Numidians. His Spanish and Celtic cavalry then wheels around and attacks the Roman center from behind. Now nearly surrounded, the normally disciplined Roman ranks fall apart and a massive slaughter ensues. Some 50,000 Romans are killed, the largest single battlefield loss in Rome's history, while Hannibal, whose victory is complete, loses only 6,000 to 7,000 men.

strongest infantry, the Africans, in the center, he held these troops in reserve on the flanks and put his less formidable Spanish and Celtic infantry in the center.

The battle opened in the usual way, with a clash of the light-armed troops from each side. Then, executing the usual manipular tactic, the Roman *hastati* closed ranks and charged the Carthaginian center. They easily pushed the enemy back. And the rest of the Romans, maintaining disciplined ranks within their lines of maniples (along with the *velites*, now arrayed in the rear), moved forward behind them, ready to enter the fight if needed. The confident Roman infantrymen had no idea that at that moment their comrades on horseback were not faring so well. Soon after the opposing cavalry units had engaged, the Carthaginian horsemen had gained the upper hand and

were now chasing the Roman horsemen off the field.

While the chase continued, Hannibal's giant deathtrap snapped shut on the unsuspecting Roman infantry. Just as he had expected, the Roman legionaries, still led by the *hastati*, drove the Carthaginian center back so far that they passed by and between his elite troops, the Africans, still standing on the flanks. These completely fresh units now turned inward and attacked. At the same time, the Carthaginian cavalry, having eliminated the Roman horsemen, wheeled around and assaulted the Romans from the rear. Surrounded, the Roman ranks crumbled. "As their outer ranks were continually cut down and the survivors were forced to pull back and huddle together," Polybius writes, "they were finally all killed where they stood. . . . So ended the battle . . . at Cannae, a struggle in which

GETTING TO KNOW ONE'S MANIPLE MATES

As pointed out here by Nathan Rosenstein, a scholar at Ohio State University at Columbus (in War and Society in the Ancient and Medieval Worlds*), besides being militarily effective, the Roman manipular system promoted camaraderie among the soldiers. And getting to know one's maniple mates made the unit more cohesive.*

The power of the Greek polis's [city-state's] phalanx lay in the strength in the bonds among its citizen hoplites, men who had long lived with one another and knew each other well. Rome was by this time [the late fourth century B.C.] no longer a simple city-state; its territory extended over much of central Italy, and public life for many citizens was mediated through the *municipia* (communities of Roman citizens who also managed their local affairs) rather than Rome itself. The men annually levied for a Roman phalanx might have little familiarity with one another and hence did not bring to war the intense mutual loyalty necessary to cohere under the pressure of combat. Breaking the phalanx into smaller blocks allowed the men of each maniple to develop a far greater degree of cohesiveness among themselves than they would have had as individuals within the mass of the phalanx.

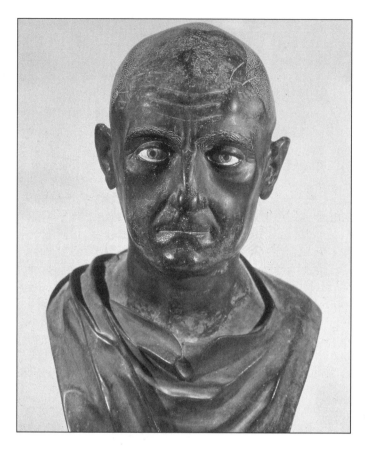

Publius Cornelius Scipio "Africanus," depicted in this surviving bust, defeated Hannibal at Zama, in north Africa, bringing the terrible Second Punic War to a close.

both victors and vanquished fought with indomitable courage."[13] Roman losses are estimated at a crippling fifty thousand, about eight times those of Hannibal.

Rome's Military Threatens the World

Despite the catastrophe at Cannae, the determined Romans rallied and held the Carthaginian invaders at bay. Moreover, Hannibal found the impact of his brilliant military successes greatly reduced when most of Rome's Italian allies remained loyal and refused to join him. Later, in 202 B.C., a reinvigorated Roman army, commanded by the talented general Publius

Cornelius Scipio, defeated Hannibal's forces at Zama, in North Africa, giving Rome a resounding victory in the war and with it control of the whole western Mediterranean sphere.

These long and danger-filled years of the first two Punic Wars challenged the Romans to increase military effectiveness once again. Especially in the latter years of the second war, the army expanded in size and became increasingly better organized. Campaigns often lasted many months or more, and newly won territories required garrisons (groups of soldiers manning forts) to hold and protect them; so the army developed a hard core of professional soldiers who signed up for hitches lasting several years. Also, out of necessity during the Punic conflicts, Rome built a powerful navy.

These same years saw people all across the Mediterranean world begin to worry. If the Roman military could defeat an empire as powerful as that of Carthage, the general reasoning went, no one in the known world was safe. That reasoning proved sound with a vengeance. Almost immediately after its second defeat of Carthage, Rome unleashed its formidable combined land and naval forces on the Greek kingdoms clustered in the Mediterranean's eastern sphere, including Macedonia (encompassing Greece and some neighboring territories), Seleucia (covering much of what are now Turkey, Palestine, and Iraq), and Egypt.

Roman Warfare Versus Greek Warfare

The crucial question was whether the Roman army, based on maniples, could overcome the widely feared phalanxes of the large Greek states. By this time the traditional phalanx, whose soldiers wielded six-foot-long spears, had given way to the Macedonian phalanx, whose men carried battle pikes up to eighteen feet or more long. The pikes of the first several rows protruded from the front, giving the formation the appearance of a gigantic porcupine with its quills erect. Polybius's often-quoted observation—that "so long as the phalanx retains it characteristic form and strength, nothing can withstand its charge or resist it face to face"[14]—was an accurate one.

Still, the Macedonian phalanx had its weaknesses. First, it was a single, solid,

BATTLE SPEECHES TO BOOST MORALE

By tradition, just prior to battle the opposing commanders of Greek and Roman armies delivered speeches designed to steel their soldiers' nerves and also to rouse their enthusiasm for the fight ahead. The actual contents of these speeches are unknown. Numerous ancient historians attempted to reconstruct them, a typical example being the second-century Greek historian Dio Cassius's version of Roman commander Mark Antony's speech preceding the Battle of Actium. (A translation of Cassius's version appears in The Roman History: The Reign of Augustus.*) Unfortunately, this and similar speeches from the works of ancient historians are at best paraphrases* based on secondhand testimony; so they should not be taken at face value. "Soldiers," said Antony (according to Dio),

All preparations for the war which it is my duty to undertake have been completed in good time. You belong to an army whose strength is as overwhelming as its quality is unsurpassed. . . . Your training has given you such a mastery of every form of combat that is known in our times that each of you, man for man, can strike fear into our adversaries. . . . If we are resolute, we shall win the greatest prizes of all; if we are careless, we shall suffer the worst of misfortunes.

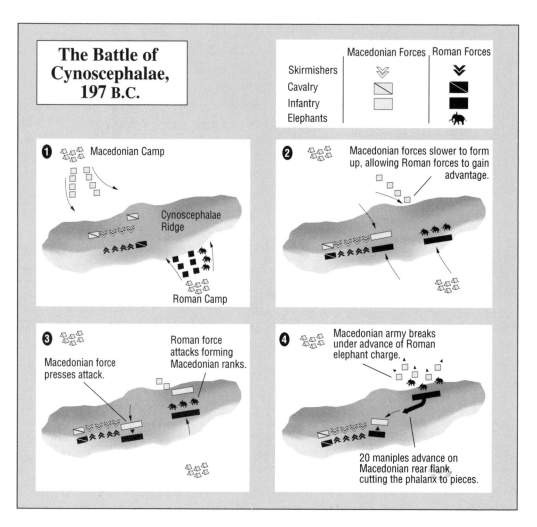

The Battle of Cynoscephalae, 197 B.C.

	Macedonian Forces	Roman Forces
Skirmishers		
Cavalry		
Infantry		
Elephants		

1 Macedonian Camp

Cynoscephalae Ridge

Roman Camp

2 Macedonian forces slower to form up, allowing Roman forces to gain advantage.

3 Macedonian force presses attack.

Roman force attacks forming Macedonian ranks.

4 Macedonian army breaks under advance of Roman elephant charge.

20 maniples advance on Macedonian rear flank, cutting the phalanx to pieces.

inflexible mass of soldiers whose separate lines and files were neither intended nor trained to act independently. Second, it was limited mainly to frontal attacks on flat ground that was largely free from obstacles. So if the phalanx was forced to fight on uneven ground or an enemy unexpectedly attacked it from the rear, it was seriously vulnerable. Sooner or later, then, a more flexible system was bound to exploit its weaknesses. As Keppie aptly puts it, "The Macedonians and Greeks, who . . . carried the phalanx to extremes of regimentation and automation, fossilized the very instrument of their former success, to their eventual downfall."[15]

The battle that foreshadowed that downfall took place at Cynoscephalae Ridge, in central Greece, in 197 B.C. The Macedonians were led by their king, Philip V, while the Roman commander was Titus Quinctius Flamininus. The two armies approached the ridge and made camp, the Macedonians to the north, the Romans to the south. The next morning each commander, unaware of the enemy's close proximity (mainly because fog blanketed the area), sent out a small covering force of skirmishers and horse-men to take control of the ridge. These forces ran into each other on the hill, a fight ensued, and in the coming hours it steadily escalated. "As the mist was clearing," Connolly explains,

THE ROMAN VICTORY AT PYDNA

The Battle of Pydna, fought near Greece's northeastern coast in the summer of 168 B.C., ended the Third Macedonian War in Rome's favor. A Roman army led by the consul Lucius Aemilius Paullus faced a phalanx commanded by Perseus, king of Macedonia. At first, the phalanx drove the Romans back. But soon the ground became uneven, hindering the Macedonian pikemen, and Paullus seized on the opportunity by ordering con-tingents of his troops into gaps that had formed in the enemy formation. Many Romans made it to the rear of the phalanx, which, assailed from front and back, quickly fell apart. Perseus lost about twenty-five thousand men and soon afterward surrendered, while Paullus lost a mere one hundred men. As at Cynoscephalae, three decades earlier, the Roman military system had proven superior to the Greek one.

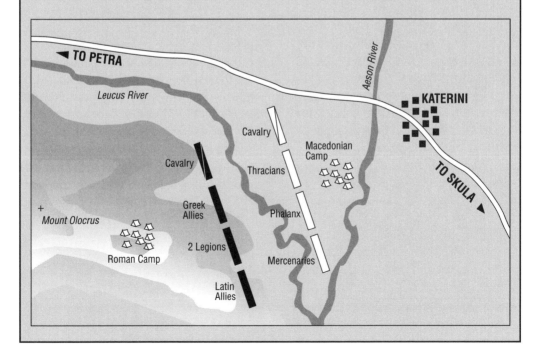

both sides now decided to bring up the rest of their forces. The Romans were nearer to the pass and managed to deploy their forces while Philip was still bringing up his. Only his right wing [i.e., the right half of his phalanx] had reached the top. . . . [His] cavalry and light-armed [troops], who were already engaged [with the Romans], were withdrawn and formed up on the right [of the phalanx]. Flamininus placed the elephants which were with his army [beasts recently acquired from Carthage in the treaty ending the Second Punic War] in front of his right wing, told his troops there to stand fast, and advanced with his left wing. Philip . . . ordered [the members of] his phalanx to lower their spears and charge. . . . The charge of the phalanx drove the legionaries back down the slope. Flamininus, seeing the imminent destruction of his left wing, threw himself at the head of the right wing and charged the Macedonian left wing, which was still forming up. The half-assembled Macedonian line crumbled before the onslaught of the ele-

phants. . . . One of the tribunes [in the Roman right wing], seizing the initiative, took 20 maniples of the *triarii*, faced about, and charged . . . into the rear of the Macedonian right wing. The action was decisive; the phalanx, unable to turn, was cut to pieces. The Romans followed up their victory, cutting down the Macedonians where they stood, even though they raised their pikes to surrender.[16]

The casualty lists were, proportionally speaking, like Cannae in reverse; Philip's losses were some 8,000 killed and 5,000 captured, while the Romans lost only 700 men.

In this battle and a few that followed, notably one fought near the Greek city of Pydna in 168 B.C., the Romans rendered the Greek military system obsolete and paved the way for Rome's absorption of the Greek lands in the coming decades. Indeed, by the end of the second century B.C., the Mediterranean Sea had become in effect a Roman lake. The nickname the Romans gave it thereafter—*mare nostrum*, "our sea"—may have been arrogant, but it was accurate.

CHAPTER THREE

The Professional Imperial Military Forces

Rome's strong, well-organized military forces and considerable expertise and vigor in prosecuting frequent wars gained it dominance over most of the Mediterranean world by the close of the second century B.C. Up to that time, the military had changed and evolved to meet new situations and needs. That process not only continued, but actually accelerated in the first century B.C., the most eventful and calamitous period the Roman people had yet endured. By the end of that century,

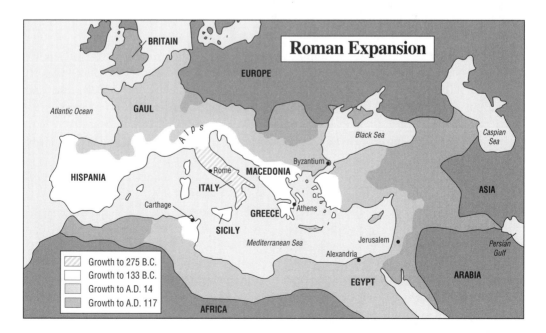

Roman Expansion

BRITAIN

EUROPE

Atlantic Ocean

GAUL

Alps

Black Sea

Caspian Sea

Byzantium

HISPANIA

Rome

MACEDONIA

ITALY

ASIA

Carthage

GREECE

Athens

SICILY

Jerusalem

Persian Gulf

Mediterranean Sea

Alexandria

ARABIA

EGYPT

AFRICA

Growth to 275 B.C.
Growth to 133 B.C.
Growth to A.D. 14
Growth to A.D. 117

This drawing is based on a bust of Gaius Marius, the first of a series of military strongmen who eventually brought the Republic to its knees.

which rocked the Republic off its foundations, they had both a new kind of government and a new array of military and paramilitary (military-like) forces, including a professional army and a fearsome regiment of bodyguards for the new leader—the emperor.

In retrospect, it is clear that this momentous series of events was a by-product of Rome's recent conquest of the Mediterranean sphere. Though impressive, such phenomenal success had come at a stiff price, one that the Romans had clearly not anticipated. In a nutshell, the problem was that the existing governmental structure was ill prepared to deal with ei-

ther a huge empire or the extremely powerful military leaders who had won it. First, the Senate, people's assembly, and other republican institutions found it increasingly difficult to administer so many diverse lands and peoples. This is hardly surprising, since the republican system had been originally designed to rule only a single people inhabiting a small city-state.

Even more ominous was the military dimension. Over the course of more than two centuries, the state had created the most formidable war machine in the known world. But government leaders had failed to develop a policy of rewarding the soldiers with substantial pensions and land when they retired. Meeting this need, the wealthiest and most powerful generals began using their influence to secure such benefits for their men. And consequently, the troops could more easily be convinced to show more allegiance to their generals than to the state.

A talented and formidable general named Gaius Marius was the first of a new breed of military strongmen to amass such a personal army, and a number of other Roman generals followed his example. Most famous of all was his nephew, Julius Caesar. The dangerous rivalries that developed among these ambitious leaders led to a series of devastating civil wars that drained the resources of the republican state and eventually caused its collapse.

The climactic battle of these conflicts took place in the waters near Actium, in western Greece, in 31 B.C. Caesar's protégé, Mark Antony, and Antony's lover/ally, Cleopatra VII, the Greek queen of Egypt, went down to defeat and soon afterward committed suicide. Four years later the now virtually powerless Senate bestowed on the victor of Actium—Caesar's adopted son, Octavian—the title of Augustus, "the

HOW ROMAN SOLDIERS WERE PAID

During much of Rome's history, the average legionary received a salary that was barely adequate to his needs. Yet the recruit could look forward to the possibility of promotion (officers received much higher pay) and various kinds of bonuses and special payments. In the Monarchy and early Republic, soldiers were not paid, since they served only on an occasional basis and made their livings from their farms. By the early fourth century B.C., however, the troops received a small daily cash payment (*stipendium*) to help cover their living expenses; and cavalrymen received money to maintain their horses when on campaign. As time went on and soldiers' terms of service lasted for years, these daily payments evolved into a regular salary, paid in three and later four installments. These payments were mostly "on paper," for most Roman soldiers did not receive their whole pay up front. First, the government deducted some money to cover the cost of armor and weapons, food,

bedding, and other expenses. Another chunk was deposited in a military bank to keep the soldiers from wasting too much on extravagant purchases. After these initial deductions, the soldier received the small amount remaining as pocket money.

The actual pay Roman soldiers received varied. In the early second century B.C., a regular legionary received 112.5 *denarii* per year. (A *denarius* was a common Roman coin.) This amount remained standard until the mid–first century B.C., when it doubled to 225 *denarii*. That figure remained standard for over a century. Then, about A.D. 84 the emperor Domitian raised the legionary's pay to 300 *denarii*, and in the early third century the emperor Caracalla upped it to 675 *denarii*. Through all these centuries, other kinds of soldiers received higher wages than regular legionaries. Centurions, for instance, earned from 3,750 to 15,000 *denarii* per year under Augustus. This means that even the lowest-paid centurion made almost seventeen times more than a regular legionary!

revered one." Though he never personally used the title of emperor, Augustus was in fact the first in the long line of dictators who ruled the political entity that became known as the Roman Empire.

Marius's Reforms

The first phase of major military reforms in this turbulent period were initiated by Caesar's uncle, Marius; he had gained tremendous power and fame for his defeat, in 102 and 101 B.C., of two large Germanic tribes that had invaded southern Europe and threatened Italy. Marius was the first Roman general to make a major move toward a true professional army.

The first question Marius addressed was that of who could become a soldier. Ever since the Servian reform, near the dawn of the Republic, the state had imposed property qualifications for service. The minimum amount of property a man had to own to serve had grown increasingly smaller in the years following the Second Punic War. But around the time Marius defeated the Germans, he helped to eliminate the property qualification and he (and then other generals) began accepting volunteers from all classes.

These developments not only greatly increased the number of potential recruits, but also initiated profound changes in the army's character. In the past the majority of soldiers, especially the well-to-do, looked on serving as a necessary but unpleasant duty. Their aim was to discharge that duty as quickly as possible and resume their civilian careers. For the volunteers of Marius's more permanent, professional force, by contrast, serving in the army *was* their career, to which many

brought enthusiasm and a sense of a purpose and pride.

Marius instituted other military reforms, including supplying all of the troops with standard weapons. Especially important in this regard was his introduction of an improved version of the *pilum*, the new one equipped with a wooden rivet that broke on impact, preventing an enemy soldier from throwing it back. Cuirasses were also more or less standard. By this time most legionaries wore versions made of mail, rows of iron rings either riveted or sewn together to form a heavy protective shirt. (Mail appears to have been invented by the Celts; the Romans adopted it shortly before the Punic Wars, although at first only well-to-do fighters could afford it.)

Marius also standardized and improved the quality of training and taught the soldiers to carry their own supplies rather than to rely on cumbersome baggage trains of mules that slowed down an army on the march. According to the first-century B.C. Greek writer Plutarch:

> There was practice in running and in long marches; and every man was compelled to carry his own baggage and to prepare his own meals. This was the origin of the expression "one of Marius's mules," applied later to any soldier who was a glutton for work and obeyed orders cheerfully and without grumbling.[17]

Maniples Replaced by Cohorts

In addition, Marius reorganized the army into cohorts, groups of about 480 men, each

These Roman legionaries of the first century B.C. lugged most of their equipment on their backs, earning them the nickname "Marius's mules."

further divided into 6 centuries of 80 men; a typical legion had 10 cohorts, or 4,800 men (although apparently it could have fewer or more men under certain conditions). Not long afterward the maniples, long the staple battlefield units, were abandoned in favor of cohorts. However, basic battlefield tactics did not change very much, for the following reasons. First, each cohort was, like a maniple, an individual unit that could act on its own. And on the battlefield, the cohorts typically formed three lines, just as the mani-

ples had. A common arrangement of a legion's ten cohorts was four in the front line and three each in the second and third lines. One line of cohorts could advance on the enemy while the cohorts of the other lines waited in reserve, as in the manipular tactic.

In fact, the cohorts were even more flexible than the maniples because they could more easily be arrayed in unusual formations. One that proved particularly effective was the "pig's head." It consisted of one cohort in front, two in the second

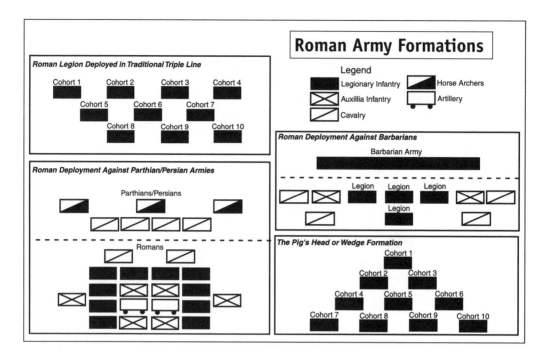

row, three in the third row, and the other four in the fourth row, together creating a massive wedge that was highly effective in frontal attacks.

The major difference between the old system and the new was the makeup of the soldiers themselves. The distinctions in armor, weapons, and tactics among the *velites*, *hastati*, *principes*, and *triarii* ceased to exist. The former *velites* donned armor and began carrying the infantry shield (*scutum*) and sword, as well as two *pila*; and the former *triarii* traded in their thrusting spears for *pila*. Well before Caesar's time, all of these kinds of fighters had become regular legionaries armed and trained in similar fashion. This highly standardized legion/cohort system and its time-proven tactics built around the formidable legionary would remain the mainstay of

the Roman military for several centuries to come.

Finally, the nature of the auxiliary troops who supported the legions changed. This was because the Roman government granted citizenship to all the residents of Italy in the 80s B.C. Since Rome's former noncitizen allies were now citizens, the *alae sociorum* ceased to exist. Thereafter, in their place, the army recruited its auxiliaries—including archers, slingers, and other light-armed troops, as well as some cavalry units—from Spain, North Africa, Germany, and other more distant lands.

Augustus and the Early Imperial Army

These military reforms of the early first century B.C. definitely produced stronger armies with many professional volunteers

JUNIOR AND SENIOR ARMY OFFICERS

Becoming an officer in the Roman army was desirable because higher rank carried with it many advantages, including better pay, more authority and respect, and increased prestige and social and political opportunities. In the imperial army, the first step up from an ordinary legionary was the position of *immunis*. The *immunes* were so named because they were immune from normal, and often unpleasant, daily military duties because they possessed special skills. An *immunis* received higher pay than a legionary and generally worked on his own and at his own pace. Among the more than one hundred kinds of *immunes* known were *agrimensores* (surveyors), *carpentarii* (carpenters), *lapidarii* (stonemasons), *librarii* (clerks), *sagittarii* (arrow makers), and *veterinarii* (veterinarians).

Above the legionaries and *immunes* were the officers, grouped into commissioned, or senior, officers, and noncommissioned, or junior, officers. The junior officers were the *tesserarius*, a sort of sergeant who made sure the legionaries were doing their jobs; the *optio*, the deputy centurion who assumed command of his century in the centurion's absence; the *signifer*, who bore the century's standards, a highly prestigious duty; and the *aquilifer*, who bore the eagle, the standard for the legion.

The lowest-ranking senior officer was the centurion, a kind of top sergeant in charge of a century. The highest-ranking and most prestigious centurion in a legion was the *primus pilus* ("first spear"), who had the right to attend meetings and strategy sessions with the six tribunes, who were ranked above the centurions in both republican and imperial legions. Above the tribunes in a republican legion (after about 190 B.C.) was the legate (*legatus*), appointed by the Senate; and above the legates were the consuls,

This modern reenactor is authentically attired as a signifer, *a legionary officer who bore his century's standard.*

until the late Republic when elected officials no longer commanded the army during their terms of office. In the early Empire, Augustus introduced the position of legionary legate, who had charge of a single legion for several years and reported directly to the general commanding the whole army (who was sometimes the emperor himself).

dedicated to serving. But in the hands of ambitious, power-hungry, often corrupt generals, such strength and dedication became instruments to use against the Roman state. When Octavian became Augustus, the first emperor, he realized that he could not hope to hold on to his newfound power while individual generals and armies ran amok. Instead, he must create an imperial army loyal to him and his new autocratic state.

To eliminate the problem of troops swearing loyalty to individual generals rather than to the state, Augustus first retained and expanded the concept of a professional army of volunteers; career men who enlisted by choice, he correctly reasoned, were more likely to support the establishment than a renegade general. He also required that soldiers swear an oath to him as their supreme commander once each year; forcing them repeatedly to re-

A drawing based on the famous Prima Porta statue of the first emperor, Augustus, who instituted a new series of military reforms.

Actium, Last Battle of the Civil Wars

The Battle of Actium, which took place in 31 B.C., was the final battle of the civil wars of the first century B.C.; its outcome signaled the last death knell of the Republic and the rise of Octavian, Julius Caesar's adopted son, as supreme ruler of the Roman realm. Octavian and his able military commander Marcus Agrippa had about 250 warships and about 80,000 land troops at their disposal. By contrast, their opponent, Roman notable Mark Antony (who was allied with Egypt's Queen Cleopatra VII), had about 60,000 infantry, 70,000 light-armed troops, and perhaps 500 or more ships. Octavian and Agrippa seized the strategic advantage by advancing on Greece while their adversaries' army and navy were still disorganized and unprepared. Before long, Antony and Cleopatra were trapped at Actium, in western Greece, and had no choice but to fight their way out. The battle took place in the nearby waters on September 2. After only two or three hours of fighting, Cleopatra suddenly fled, followed soon afterward by Antony. It is likely that the two had planned their escape from the beginning, their main objective being to save the treasure they carried and use it to raise new forces and continue prosecuting the war. Whatever the reason for their flight, the move threw their remaining ships and men into disarray. Antony's forces were shattered, and the dawn of a new Roman world was at hand.

new the vow was a way of reestablishing the tradition of a soldier's primary loyalty to the state. In addition, and perhaps most importantly, he granted them hefty bonuses and created a system of land grants as part of their pensions, making it almost impossible for a general to buy their allegiance.

Augustus's new reforms also altered the size and command structure of the military. The standing army was now composed of 28 legions, each with about 5,500 men (counting cavalry), for a total of more than 150,000 men. By the end of Augustus's reign, each legion was commanded by an officer called a legionary legate (*legatus legionis*), who was appointed by the emperor; under the legate were the traditional six tribunes; and under them were the centurions (each in charge of a single century).

More Rounded, Rigorous Training

In addition to such large-scale reforms, the new imperial system focused on the individual Roman legionary, who became more formidable than ever. Roman soldiers had long been highly flexible, with the ability to adapt quickly to changing situations. Even before Marius's time, Polybius had written:

Every Roman soldier, once he is armed and goes into action, can adapt himself equally well to any place or time and meet an attack from any quarter. He is likewise equally well-prepared and needs to make no change whether he has to fight with the main body [of the army] or with a detachment . . . or singly. Accordingly, since the effective use of the parts of the Roman army is so much superior, their plans are much more likely to achieve success than those of others.[18]

One important key to this success was a high degree of training. In the late Republic, according to Polybius, a typical week for new recruits was as follows. On the first day the soldiers had to run about 3.7 miles in full armor, an extremely arduous feat; on day two they cleaned and polished their weapons and underwent an exacting inspection; on day three they rested; on day four they endured relentless weapons drills—practicing sword play, spear throwing, and the like; on day five they ran another 3.7 miles in armor; on day six they had another inspection; and on day seven they rested again. The following week they repeated the process.

After Augustus's reforms, the training became even more wide ranging and rigorous. During the early Empire, new recruits learned to march by engaging in exhausting parade drills twice a day until they were able to cover twenty-four miles in just five hours while wearing full armor. Next, they had to march mile after grueling mile, day after day, carrying a full pack consisting of some sixty pounds of weapons, tools, and rations. They also learned how to build a camp, ride a horse, and swim. Then came weapons training. According to Vegetius, a late fourth-century Roman civil servant who wrote a handbook on military matters, the trainers

made round wickerwork shields, twice as heavy as those of service weight, and gave their recruits wooden staves [sticks] instead of swords, and these again were of double weight. With these they were made to practice at the stakes both morning and afternoon. . . . A stake was planted in the ground by each recruit, in such a manner that it projected six feet in height and could not sway. Against this stake the recruit practiced . . . just as if he were fighting a real enemy. Sometimes he aimed as against the head or the face, sometimes he threatened from the flanks [sides], sometimes he endeavored to strike down the knees and the legs. He gave ground, he attacked, he assaulted, and he assailed the stake with all the skill and energy required in actual fighting . . . and in this exercise care was taken to see that the recruit did not rush forward so rashly to inflict a wound as to lay himself open to a counterstroke from any quarter. Furthermore, they learned to strike, not with the edge [of the sword], but with the point. For those who strike with the edge have not only been beaten by the Romans quite easily, but they have even been laughed at.[19]

Alternating with such drills were others featuring throwing spears, as well as forced marches, long runs in armor, and practice at jumping and felling trees. Eventually, the recruits lined up in an open field and practiced shaping the various common battle formations until they

A legionary centurion (above, center) was easily distinguished by his transverse helmet crest and vine stick; the reenactors at right portray legionaires training with wicker shield and wooden swords.

could do so quickly and precisely. And finally, they engaged in mock battles, in which the points of their swords and javelins were covered to prevent serious injuries.

This extensive and rigorous training regimen shows that the Romans took war and soldiering very seriously. Indeed, failure, whether in training or on the battlefield, was not an option. "So strict was the attention paid to training," Vegetius writes,

that weapons training instructors received double rations, and soldiers who had failed to reach an adequate standard in those exercises were compelled to receive their rations in barley [a grain then considered inferior to wheat] instead of wheat. The wheat ration

was not restored to them until they had demonstrated by practical tests, in the presence of the . . . tribunes or the senior officers, that they were proficient in every branch of their military studies.[20]

Two Motivations for Warfare

The early imperial Roman legionary was the most remarkable and rounded soldier the world had ever seen. On the one hand, his discipline, courage, determination, and flexibility, coupled with his excellent training

Roman cavalry of the early Empire. Note the long shields to protect both rider and horse and the lack of stirrups, which had not yet been invented.

and the superior strategy and tactics of his commanders, made him the world's first truly professional warrior. And as such, he was often a highly efficient killing machine.

The imperial troops were far from merely brutish, ruthless destroyers, however. In their conquests, they often carried with them a powerful civilizing influence in the form of Roman administration, law and order, architecture, literature, and other cultural aspects. Scholar Michael Simkins points out:

> The Roman soldier was . . . the primary agent for the propagation of Roman ideas and the establishment of a settled way of life. . . . Though the initial shock of conquest and the often unjust treatment of the subjugated nation must seem unacceptable behavior to many people today, it is all too easy to overlook the fact that a good proportion of those brought so roughly within the Roman pale [sphere], settled down . . . and flourished. Some became Roman citizens themselves, by military service in . . . Rome's forces; others by services rendered to the Empire in a variety of ways. . . . Citizenship was hereditary and carried with it substantial benefits under the Roman system.[21]

It was with the "one-two punch," so to speak, of military aggression and the spread of culture that Rome first conquered and then absorbed most of southern and central Britain in the first century A.D. The campaigns of the emperor Trajan in southern Germany in the early second century witnessed a similar process. In the view of most of the early emperors, warfare had two aims, one political, the other altruistic in nature; it was a means not only of making the realm larger, but also of bestowing the "blessings" of Roman civilization on "barbarians" who lacked them.

Other Imperial Armed Forces

Besides the professional army that, with minor modifications, served the Empire for nearly three centuries, Augustus created some smaller paramilitary forces whose members were also paid professionals. Originally they were conceived as special garrisons for the capital city, but they also came to be used in other cities. One was a force of unusually well-paid troops called the Praetorian Guard. Its membership was at first restricted to men of Italian birth, and its primary tasks were to guard the emperor and see that his orders and policies were enforced.

The original Praetorian force consisted of 9 cohorts, each having from 500 to 1,000 men, for a total of about 5,000 or so. (Later emperors considerably increased its size.) Some patrolled the Palatine Hill (where Augustus lived) and other parts of Rome, while others were stationed in surrounding towns. Their leader was called the Praetorian Prefect.

The Praetorians had armor and weapons very similar, if not more or less identical, to those of Roman legionaries—metal cuirasses and helmets, and sword and javelin carried on the right side. In the early Empire, both Praetorians and legionaries began using a new kind of cuirass. Called *lorica segmentata*, it consisted of about two dozen thin strips of

ERECTING A ROMAN ARMY CAMP

The first-century A.D. *Jewish historian Josephus's account of the building of a Roman army camp, excerpted here from his* The Jewish War, *is quite similar to that of the Greek historian Polybius, who wrote over two centuries earlier.*

Whenever they [the Romans] invade hostile territory they rigidly refuse battle till they have fortified their camp. This they do not construct haphazardly or unevenly, nor do they tackle the job . . . without organized squads; if the ground is uneven it is thoroughly leveled, then the site is marked out as a rectangle. To this end, the army is followed by a large number of engineers with all the tools needed for building. The inside is divided up, ready for the huts. From outside, the perimeter looks like a wall and is equipped with towers evenly spaced. In the gaps between the towers they mount [mechanical] spear-throwers, catapults, stone-throwers . . . all ready to be discharged. Four gates are constructed, one in each length of wall, practicable for the entry of baggage-animals and wide enough for armed sorties [detachments of combat troops], if called for. The camp is divided up by streets, accurately marked out; in the middle are erected the officers' huts, and in the middle of these the commander's headquarters, which resembles a shrine. It all seems like a mushroom town, with marketplace, workmen's quarters, and orderly-rooms.

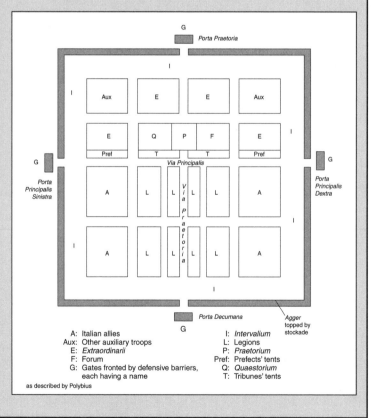

A: Italian allies
Aux: Other auxiliary troops
E: *Extraordinarii*
F: Forum
G: Gates fronted by defensive barriers, each having a name

I: *Intervalium*
L: Legions
P: *Praetorium*
Pref: Prefects' tents
Q: *Quaestorium*
T: Tribunes' tents

as described by Polybius

Two Roman legionaries of the early Empire sport typical gear of their day: lorica segmentata *armor, the heavy* pilum, *the* gladius *(worn on the right side), the rectangular* scutum, *and short leather boots* (caligulae).

laminated iron held together with small hinges, buckles, hooks, and/or leather straps. One possible difference between Praetorian and legionary equipment was the shield; some evidence suggests that the Praetorians carried the old oval *scutum*, while the legionaries wielded the more modern rectangular version.

Beginning in the reign of Augustus's successor, Tiberius, the Praetorians became more of a political force in its own right, as its leaders and members inter-

vened in imperial affairs at will, usually when paid to do so by one ambitious faction or another. In A.D. 41, for example, the Praetorians joined in the conspiracy to kill the third emperor, Caligula; and they then placed Claudius on the throne. In an even more audacious display, following the assassination of the emperor Commodus in 192, the Guards murdered his successor, Pertinax, after a reign of only eighty-seven days because he had paid them only half of a promised bonus;

This drawing is based on a relief sculpture showing a group of Praetorian Guards. At times these elite soldiers assassinated some of the emperors they were charged to protect.

they then auctioned off the throne to the highest bidder.

Another paramilitary force created by Augustus consisted of the urban cohorts (*cohortes urbanae*), units of policemen for the city of Rome. There were three cohorts, each having a thousand men commanded by a tribune, who reported to the Urban Prefect (the official who ran the city for the emperor). The urban cohorts were stationed in barracks on the Viminal Hill (until the late third century A.D., when their headquarters moved to the Campus Martius, the region comprising the city's eastern sector). A normal hitch for members of these units was twenty years, and they received considerably better pay than ordinary legionaries. Over time other cities in the realm instituted their own urban cohorts.

Still other imperial forces who were allowed to wield weapons like army soldiers were the *vigiles*, members of a permanent professional firefighting brigade set up in the city of Rome by Augustus about A.D. 6. They were divided into 7 cohorts of 500 (later 1,000) men each. A tribune commanded each cohort and these 7 men reported to a prefect. In addition to fighting fires, the *vigiles* had several law-enforcement duties. After the emperor Nero instituted fire-safety regulations in the 60s A.D., they inspected tenement blocks and other buildings to make sure the citizens were complying with the fire laws. Some *vigiles* also acted as community policemen who patrolled the dark, dangerous streets of the capital at night. They carried swords and rods (like modern police nightsticks), and they could arrest muggers and other wrongdoers and turn them over to the office of the Urban Prefect. Other cities and towns eventually set up their own brigades of *vigiles* (though on a smaller scale than those in Rome).

Thus, whether in the form of regular army troops, imperial guards, or brigades of city police and firemen, military regimentation and methods permeated all levels and niches of Roman society. This is hardly surprising considering that Rome was a nation and empire born out of, shaped by, and maintained through warfare.

CHAPTER FOUR

Fortifications and Siege Warfare

In Roman legend, Romulus built a wall to protect the new city named after him; in the Empire's final years, wave after wave of so-called barbarian tribes overran the vast Roman realm's many border forts and walls. These were only the beginning and end of Rome's obvious need for and almost constant preoccupation with defensive measures, which constituted a crucial aspect of their warfare. Indeed, the Romans became renowned for their defensive walls, like those built to protect the capital or the one Hadrian erected across northern Britain; their highly fortified army camps; and their stone forts, the direct predecessors of medieval castles.

Most Roman troops, including those stationed in distant provinces or on the Empire's frontiers, remained on the *de*fensive side of fortifications. However, some found themselves on the *of*fensive side. These were the soldiers who engaged in siege warfare—surrounding and capturing enemy fortresses and towns. As Peter Connolly points out, "Fortifications and siege warfare are inextricably [inescapably] combined. The development of one inevitably stimulates changes in the other,"[22] and therefore the two must be considered together. Even the largely calm *Pax Romana*, the roughly two-century-long era of peace and prosperity inaugurated by Augustus, saw its share of such sieges. (The most famous and dramatic of these took place in Palestine when the Jews rebelled against Rome in the late 60s and early 70s A.D.) The Romans did not invent most of the siege techniques they employed; rather, in their usual manner, they borrowed the ideas from others and then applied them in the ways that best suited their own needs.

Barriers Designed to Keep Enemies Out

During the era of the Roman Monarchy and early Republic, there were no distant provinces or frontiers to defend. Evidence uncovered by archaeologists shows that some of the original seven hills of Rome were fortified by mounds of earth topped by stockade fences and fronted by ditches, similar to the outer defenses of later Roman marching camps. The residents apparently relied on these simple barriers, along with the steepness of the hills, to discourage large-scale attacks.

Later, in 378 B.C., the Romans began work on the so-called Servian Wall, a more formidable stone barrier that ran around the city's entire perimeter. It was backed (and strengthened) by an enormous rampart of earth and fronted by a wide, deep ditch or moat. As time went on and Rome's territory expanded, other Roman cities, as well as forts, were protected by similar protective barriers.

The only significant innovation the Romans made in the art of fortification during the remainder of the Republic and early Empire was the portcullis, which later became a familiar feature of medieval castles. This was a heavy door, usually made of wood, and shod with iron for extra strength, that protected a wall or fortress's gateway. A system of ropes and winches located in a chamber above raised and lowered the door. The fourth-century B.C. Greek writer Aeneas Tacticus gave this description of a version of his own time:

> If a large number of the enemy come in . . . and you wish to catch them you should have ready above the

Children play in the ruins of the military fort at Vindolanda, near Hadrian's Wall in north-central Britain. Parts of the fort, including a wooden gatehouse, have been reconstructed.

center of the gateway a gate of the strongest possible timber overlaid with iron. Then when you wish to cut off [part of] the enemy [forces] as they rush in, you should let this drop down and the gate itself will not only as it falls destroy some of them, but will also keep the [rest of] the foe from entering, while at the same time the forces on the wall are shooting at the enemy at the gate.[23]

By the early second century A.D., the Romans had come to perceive a need to fortify not just individual cities and forts, but the realm as a whole. So they began building defensive walls, fortresses, and forts in larger numbers and on a grander scale than ever before. The most spectacular surviving example of a fortification wall meant to keep enemies out of Roman territory is Hadrian's Wall, begun in 122.

In its heyday, it stretched for some seventy-three miles across the north-central section of the province of Britain (conquered by the Romans in the previous century). According to Durham University scholar Brian Dobson:

This stone wall was perhaps some 5 meters [16 feet] high, fronted with a broad berm [space between the ditch and the wall] and a ditch 8 meters [26 feet] wide and 3 meters [10 feet] deep. It was defended by eighty small mile-castles about 1,500 meters [a Roman mile, slightly less than a modern mile] apart and some 160 turrets [defensive towers]. Two turrets were placed between each mile-castle about 500 meters [1,640 feet] apart. . . . There were gateways at 1,600 meter intervals, though the majority of these seem in time to

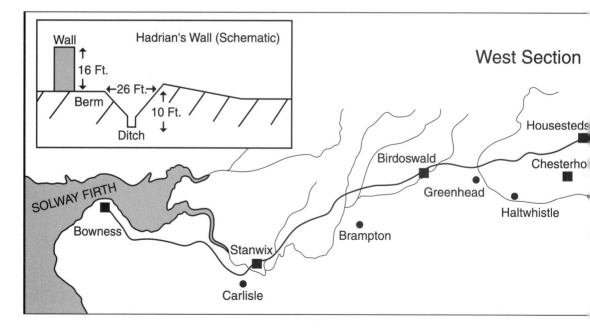

have been narrowed to passages for people on foot.[24]

Beginning in about 140, Hadrian's successor, Antoninus Pius (reigned 138–161) erected a similar but smaller wall several miles north of Hadrian's. The new fortification was intended to replace the old one and guard an expanded Roman frontier. But about six or seven decades later, the Romans abandoned the Antonine Wall and fell back to the one Hadrian had built.

Fortified Military Bases

Running behind Hadrian's and Antoninus's walls were roads along which forts were erected at intervals; these forts served as quarters for most of the soldiers who manned the walls. In the case of Hadrian's Wall, the forts were spaced about six miles apart. Beginning in the late first century, the Romans constructed a much larger network of forts linked by roads along the frontiers near the Rhine and Danube Rivers, which separated Roman and Germanic lands. Significantly reinforced and expanded by Hadrian in the second century, this defensive line stretched for some twenty-five hundred miles, from the North Sea in the northwest to the Black Sea in the east. And it later became the basis for an even more formidable network of frontier defenses installed by the emperor Diocletian and his successors in the late third and early fourth centuries. The forts were eventually spaced about five to six miles apart (or closer in some places); and between them loomed numerous solidly built, freestanding, square-shaped watchtowers measuring twenty to forty feet on a side; there were also intermittent sections of stockades and ditches, all guarded by sentries.

The next level of defense consisted of a system of fortresses that backed up the

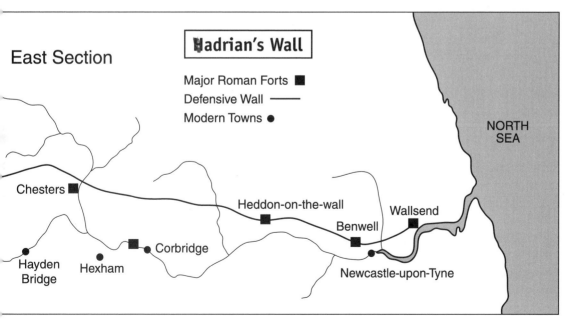

East Section

Hadrian's Wall

Major Roman Forts ■
Defensive Wall ——
Modern Towns ●

NORTH SEA

Chesters ■

Heddon-on-the-wall ■

Wallsend ■

Benwell ■

Corbridge ●

Hayden Bridge ●

Hexham ●

Newcastle-upon-Tyne ●

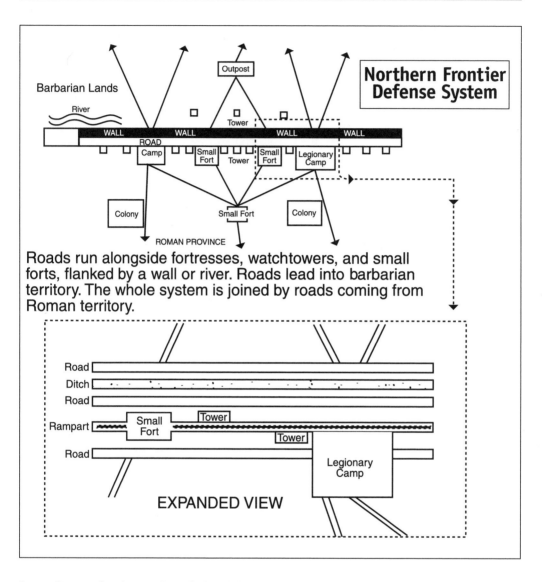

Northern Frontier Defense System

Roads run alongside fortresses, watchtowers, and small forts, flanked by a wall or river. Roads lead into barbarian territory. The whole system is joined by roads coming from Roman territory.

EXPANDED VIEW

forts. One major factor that distinguished the fortresses from the forts was their size. Generally, the forts were relatively small—each covering about two to fourteen acres and accommodating a few hundred to perhaps a thousand men. Fortresses, by comparison, were much larger. Each covered fifty or more acres and housed at least one legion, up to five thousand or more men.

There were obviously fewer fortresses than forts at any given time.

Size differences aside, Roman forts and fortresses, which can be classified together as fortified military bases, had much in common. First, both were structurally similar, being more permanent versions of the traditional and temporary Roman marching camp. Like marching camps, permanent bases had outer defenses, including ramparts and ditches. However, the defenses of the bases were much more elaborate, like those of fortified towns, including towers at intervals in the walls and wider and deeper moats.

Living on a Military Base

In fact, the permanent military bases had many of the amenities of small Roman towns. Such a base had streets arranged in a grid pattern (as in a marching camp). It also featured blocks of barracks, at first of timber and later of stone, in place of the marching camp's tents. Each block had ten or eleven sets of double rooms, each of which housed a unit of eight men. Of the two rooms, the main one, about fifteen feet square, was for sleeping, while a somewhat smaller one provided storage for the men's equipment.

At the end of each block of barracks was a centurion's quarters. Because of his rank and prestige, a centurion had eight or nine rooms, including a latrine and washroom, arranged around a central corridor. (Some of these chambers were probably offices and storerooms; and it is possible that his *optio* shared the quarters with him.) Tribunes had their own separate

The ruins of the bathhouse in the Roman fort at Chesters, located on the south side of Hadrian's Wall.

65

houses, equipped with kitchens, dining rooms, and suites for their personal staffs.

Also like a town, a military base had various civilized amenities. These included bathhouses, introduced into legionary fortresses in the first century A.D. Later, some forts also featured bathhouses, smaller in scale of course, most often located just outside the walls. Unlike the relatively simple modern bath or shower, says former University of Birmingham scholar Graham Webster, the Roman method of bathing

demanded a series of rooms of varying temperatures and humidity which induced a perspiration subsequently sluiced [washed] off by warm or cold water, followed by massage and oils rubbed into the body. It must have been an exhilarating experience and its effect on the morale of the troops very considerable.[25]

Much more than a mere bathing facility, however, a Roman bathhouse was a place in which people exercised, played sports, gam-

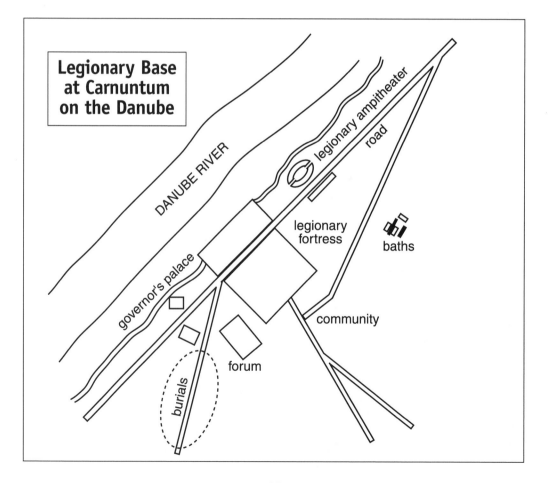

Legionary Base at Carnuntum on the Danube

DANUBE RIVER

legionary ampitheater

road

legionary fortress

baths

governor's palace

community

burials

forum

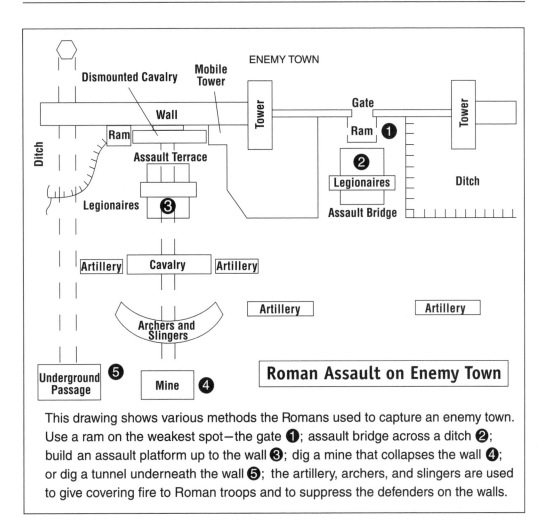

Roman Assault on Enemy Town

This drawing shows various methods the Romans used to capture an enemy town. Use a ram on the weakest spot—the gate ❶; assault bridge across a ditch ❷; build an assault platform up to the wall ❸; dig a mine that collapses the wall ❹; or dig a tunnel underneath the wall ❺; the artillery, archers, and slingers are used to give covering fire to Roman troops and to suppress the defenders on the walls.

bled, read, and socialized; and it is a good bet that a soldier spent a good deal of his time in the local bathhouse when his daily shift was over.

Off-duty servicemen no doubt also frequented their local amphitheaters (arenas with wooden or stone seating, like the Colosseum in Rome) in those bases that had them. From the second century on, small amphitheaters were erected outside the walls of many of the fortresses (the forts generally being too small to merit such luxuries). One of these, excavated at Caerleon, in southwestern Britain, measures about 265 by 220 feet and in its prime sat an estimated six thousand, well more than the complement of an average legion. A few such arenas were even larger, although most were probably a bit smaller. They were only occasionally used for staging gladiator and wild animal fights, since these shows were very expensive to stage and were rarely seen outside of Rome and other large cities.

Less expensive sorts of entertainment, such as boxing, trained animal acts, and pantomimes may have been presented a bit more often. For the most part, though, such activities as campwide religious ceremonies, group exercise, and military drills took place in these arenas.

In addition to housing, baths, and in some cases an amphitheater, a military base had many other kinds of buildings. These included administrative offices, a hospital, granaries, a prison, an officers' club, and some shops and taverns. It appears that the soldiers were not the only ones who patronized the baths, shops, and other facilities. Recent excavations of a Roman fort at Vindolanda, just south of Hadrian's Wall in northern Britain, have revealed that some women used the base bathhouse (lying just outside the fort's walls). They seem to have been the wives and daughters of base officers. These women probably lived in a nearby civilian settlement and visited the base on a regular basis, enjoying its social life. (It is unknown whether the wives and girl-friends of ordinary soldiers were allowed this same privilege.)

Surrounding an Enemy Town

Naturally, such amenities and leisure pursuits were to a great extent curtailed during periods when a base's soldiers were engaged in actual warfare. At such times, these men were all business. And the same is certainly true of those Roman troops who fought on the other side of a fort's or town's walls, as attackers and besiegers. Very little is known about Roman siege warfare before the time of the Punic Wars. According to later ancient historians, the Romans besieged the Etruscan city of Veii in the late fifth century B.C. and finally captured it by digging a tunnel under its walls; however, most details of the siege remain uncertain.

The first Roman siege for which details *are* known was that of the Sicilian town of Agrigentum in 262 B.C., at the start of the First Punic War. Here, the besiegers used a technique that became the standard Roman siege system. This was circumvalla-

THE PROUD AVERNI DEFY ROME

The Gauls Julius Caesar besieged at Alesia in 52 B.C. were Averni (or Arverni) tribesmen. They had became quite prominent by the mid–second century B.C., at which time they dominated much of central Gaul. Long bitter enemies of their neighbors the Aedui, the Averni fought against an alliance of Aedui and Romans, who delivered them a debilitating defeat in 121 B.C. Subsequently, Averni territory shrank and the Aedui became dominant in the region. During Julius Caesar's Gallic campaigns in the 50s B.C., the proud Averni made one last bid for supremacy under their talented war chief Vercingetorix. However, Caesar soundly defeated them. And over time they became romanized, along with the other Gallic peoples.

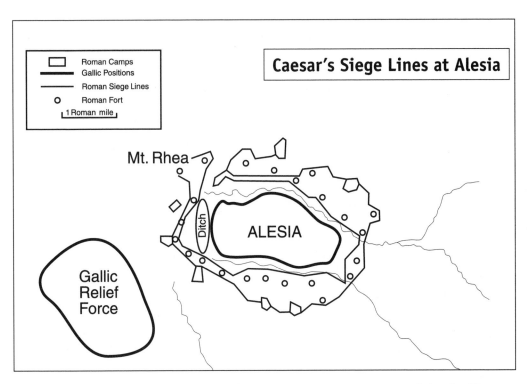

Caesar's Siege Lines at Alesia

☐	Roman Camps
▬	Gallic Positions
—	Roman Siege Lines
○	Roman Fort

tion, basically blockading a town or fort by surrounding it. According to Connolly:

Several camps would be established around the besieged town at some distance from it. These would be joined by lines of trenches and [earthen] ramparts cutting the town off from the surrounding country and preventing anyone from escaping. If there was no enemy army in the field this would be sufficient, but if there was any possibility of relief from the outside, a second line of ramparts and ditches [bicircumvallation] would be established facing outwards. Between the two lines there was a broad thoroughfare [roadway], often several meters wide, facilitating rapid troop move-

ments to any part of the fortifications. Forts and picket [sentry] posts were placed at intervals along the whole circuit so that every point of the line was watched.[26]

This was the method Julius Caesar employed in his famous siege of the Gallic fortress of Alesia in 52 B.C. Because the fearless Gauls repeatedly sent out warriors to harass the Roman soldiers guarding the perimeter, he thought it prudent to make some additions to the usual ramparts, ditches, and guard posts. In that way, he recorded in his surviving personal log, the *Commentaries on the Gallic Wars,*

our lines could be defended by a smaller number of men. Tree trunks or very stout branches were cut down

At the epic siege of Alesia, in 52 B.C., Julius Caesar's troops construct the inner ring of their siege circumvallation around the town, which can be seen in the distance.

and the ends were stripped of bark and sharpened; long trenches, five feet deep, were dug and into these the stakes were sunk and fastened at the bottom so that they could not be torn up, while the top part projected above the surface. There were five rows of them in each trench, fastened and interlaced together in such a way that anyone who got among them would impale himself on the sharp points. The soldiers called them "tombstones." In front of these, arranged in diagonal lines forming quincunxes, we dug pits three feet deep and tapering downward toward the bottom. Smooth stakes as thick as a man's thigh, hardened by fire and with sharp points, were fixed in these pits and set so as not to project more than about three inches from the ground. To keep them firmly in place, the earth was trodden down hard to a depth of one foot and the rest of the pit was filled with twigs and brushwood so as to conceal the trap. These traps were set in groups, each of which contained eight rows three feet apart. The men called them "lilies" from their resemblance to that flower. In front of these was another defensive device. Blocks of wood a foot long with iron hooks fixed in them were buried underneath the surface and thickly scattered all over the area. They were called "spurs" by the soldiers. When these defenses were completed, I constructed another line of fortifications of the same kind, but this time facing the other way, against the enemy from the outside. These additional fortifications had a circuit of thirteen miles.[27]

Caesar's siege of Alesia was ultimately successful, as he was able simultaneously to defeat the Gauls within the fortress and an even larger force that attacked the outer perimeter of his defenses.

Dogged Persistence Wins the Day

Caesar and his men expended a considerable amount of time and energy sealing off the Alesia fortress. This clearly illustrates the difference between Roman siege techniques and those of the Greeks, from whom the

Modern reconstructions of two versions of Roman artillery. The ballista, *or "stone caster" (top) could hurl small rocks as far as 300 yards; cocking the mechanism of the* onager, *a catapult (below), required seven or eight men.*

Romans learned the basics of the art of siege warfare. In the Republic's last few centuries, the Greeks developed numerous clever, sophisticated, and often enormous siege machines. These included giant drills that could pierce stone walls and monstrous siege towers that moved on rollers and held dozens of catapults and other mechanical missile throwers (artillery). The Romans also employed siege towers and artillery. However, their versions were generally smaller and used less frequently. More often, they preferred to exploit the nearly limitless muscle power of the thousands of soldiers making up their legions. The soldiers took weeks or even months to build the kind of elaborate defenses and booby traps Caesar employed at Alesia; or to erect gigantic earthen ramps or long underground tunnels to gain access to the town or fortress they were besieging. In almost every Roman siege, therefore, dogged persistence and patience, along with sheer manpower, won the day.

Among the largest and most impressive and devastating of these sieges were three conducted by the Romans in the province of Judaea (in Palestine) during the Jewish rebellion lasting from 66 to 73. First to fall, after fifty days of relentless pressure, was the town of Jotapata, commanded by the Jewish historian Josephus. (Captured by the Romans, Josephus went on to desert the Jewish cause, to become a Roman citizen, and eventually to compile his now-famous detailed account of the war.)

The ancient and revered great Jewish Temple of Solomon burns during the months-long Roman siege of Jerusalem in A.D. 70, as depicted by the Renaissance Italian artist Ercole de Roberti.

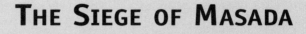

THE SIEGE OF MASADA

One of the most famous sieges of ancient times, that of the Jewish fortress of Masada, proved a classic demonstration of the Roman approach to siege warfare, combining methodical patience, enormous muscle power, and a huge siege ramp. In A.D. 71, after the general collapse of the Jewish revolt that had begun almost five years before, a few militant diehards retreated to Masada, perched on the summit of an imposing rock plateau overlooking the western shore of the Dead Sea. There, the leader of the group, Eleazar ben Ya'ir, and some 960 men, women, and children bravely determined to resist Rome to their dying breath.

In 72 the new Roman military governor, Flavius Silva, set about capturing Masada. He had two full legions (ten thousand men) and several thousand Jewish prisoners, whom he used to create a vast supply train of men and mules to carry food, water, timber, and equipment into the desert to prosecute the siege. Silva first surrounded the plateau with a six-foot-thick stone wall having guard towers spaced at intervals of about eighty to one hundred yards. Then he constructed a huge assault ramp (of earth and stone, reinforced by large timbers) on Masada's western slope. Once the ramp was finished and the attackers had breached walls, they received an unexpected and eerie surprise. All of the defenders (except for two women and five children) had killed themselves in a suicide pact, preferring death to surrender.

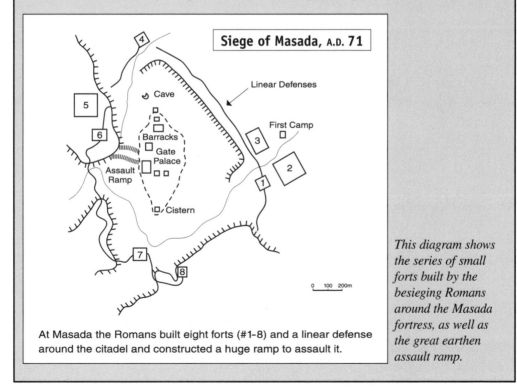

At Masada the Romans built eight forts (#1–8) and a linear defense around the citadel and constructed a huge ramp to assault it.

This diagram shows the series of small forts built by the besieging Romans around the Masada fortress, as well as the great earthen assault ramp.

The larger and more destructive siege of Jerusalem began in the early spring of 70. Applying their usual methodical methods of circumvallation, earthen ramps, and underground tunnels, by May the Romans had made it past the first of the city's three defensive walls. Late in August they reached the Jews' great sacred Temple. In spite of the desire of the Roman commander (the future emperor Titus) that the building be spared, it caught fire and was destroyed. Fierce fighting continued and the attackers were unable to capture the entire city until late September. What they did not burn, they demolished later; and there was much indiscriminate killing and plundering by Roman troops.

When Jerusalem fell, most of the insurrection collapsed. About a thousand diehard rebels retreated to the fortress of Masada, on a steep hill in the desert. And despite resolute resistance, the construction of an enormous earthen siege ramp enabled the Romans to capture it in 72. The cold reality was that, no matter how brave the defenders, no city or fortress in the known world could keep the Romans out if they wanted to get in.

CHAPTER FIVE

Naval Weapons and Tactics

The Romans did not start out as a seafaring people, as the Phoenicians and Carthaginians did. So Rome did not build and maintain any significant number of warships during the years of the Monarchy and early Republic. But when the Romans saw the pressing need for such ships, they constructed them with astonishing speed. In their first war with Carthage (264–241 B.C.), they managed the phenomenal accomplishment of building some 120 fully equipped warships in only sixty days. This feat, Polybius exclaimed,

> illustrates better than any other the extraordinary spirit and audacity of the Romans. . . . It was not a question of having adequate resources for the enterprise, for they had in fact none whatsoever, nor had they ever given a thought to the sea before this. But once they had conceived the idea, they embarked on it so boldly that without waiting to

gain any experience in naval warfare they immediately engaged [joined battle with] the Carthaginians, who had for generations enjoyed an unchallenged supremacy at sea.[28]

Yet even after building its first navy and defeating Carthage's fleets, Rome did not act or think like a traditional naval power. As noted historian Lionel Casson puts it, the Romans were "an anomaly in maritime history, a race of [land]lubbers who became lords of the sea in spite of themselves."[29] In fact, Rome's military tradition as a land power was so ingrained that its navy was long seen as secondary to and considerably less prestigious than the army. And for centuries most young Roman men aspired to be soldiers rather than sailors. One young second-century A.D. naval recruit wrote home:

> God willing, I hope to be transferred to the army. But nothing will

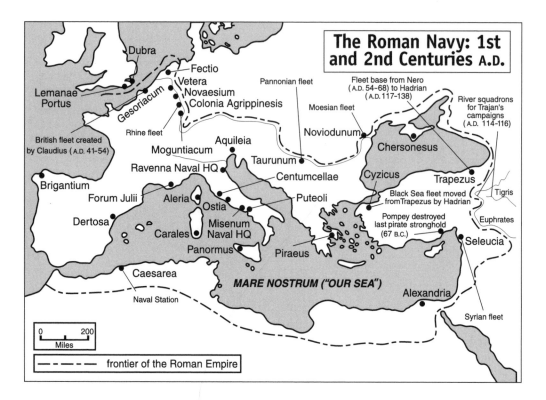

The Roman Navy: 1st and 2nd Centuries A.D.

Dubra
Fectio
Vetera
Novaesium
Colonia Agrippinesis
Lemanae Portus
Gesoriacum
Pannonian fleet
Moesian fleet
Fleet base from Nero (A.D. 54–68) to Hadrian (A.D. 117–138)
River squadrons for Trajan's campaigns (A.D. 114-116)
Rhine fleet
British fleet created by Claudius (A.D. 41-54)
Moguntiacum
Aquileia
Noviodunum
Chersonesus
Taurunum
Ravenna Naval HQ
Centumcellae
Cyzicus
Trapezus
Brigantium
Forum Julii
Aleria
Puteoli
Black Sea fleet moved from Trapezus by Hadrian
Tigris
Dertosa
Ostia
Misenum Naval HQ
Pompey destroyed last pirate stronghold (67 B.C.)
Euphrates
Carales
Panormus
Piraeus
Seleucia
Caesarea
MARE NOSTRUM ("OUR SEA")
Alexandria
Naval Station
Syrian fleet

0   200
Miles

– – – – –   frontier of the Roman Empire

be done around here without money [to bribe persons in a position to facilitate the transfer?], and letters of recommendation will be no good unless a man helps himself.[30]

The oarsmen and other crewmen who manned Rome's warships were mostly noncitizens or foreigners. (Contrary to depictions in some Hollywood films, the rowers were not slaves, nor were they chained to their oars.) During republican times, most of these seamen were members of Rome's Italian allies, while during the Empire they came primarily from Greece, Phoenicia, Egypt, Syria, and other lands with long-established seafaring traditions. Their main incentive for signing on for their grueling twenty-six-year

hitches was to be granted Roman citizenship as a reward on discharge.

Despite the fact that Roman sailors served in what most people viewed as the inferior branch of the service, the navy and its personnel had important, sometimes even vital duties and responsibilities to perform. Chief among these, of course, was fighting enemy navies when the need arose. Though these clashes rarely decided the outcome of a war, now and then they did, as in the case of the First Punic War or the civil conflict between Octavian and Antony. Also, the ships carried consuls, governors, emperors, and other high officials (and sometimes contingents of land troops) to faraway locations much faster than was possible over land. In addition, sailors carried crucial military dispatches during both wartime and peacetime; served as policemen in commercial ports and on the rivers flowing near the frontiers; chased and sank pirate vessels that threatened commercial shipping; guarded the grain supplies in Rome and later in Egypt and other provinces; and worked on civil engineering projects, including raising and lowering the giant awning that protected Rome's great amphitheater, the Colosseum.

Rome's Navy Through the Centuries

The first known instance in which Roman warships and sailors performed such duties occurred in 311 B.C. when the government funded the building of a handful of small craft to patrol the waters of western Italy and keep them secure from pirates who had been raiding the area. Some twenty years later, a group of these Roman ships got into a fight with the larger, more formidable war fleet of the independent Greek city of Taras (Tarentum in Latin), on Italy's southern coast. The Romans suffered such a decisive defeat that they beached their remaining ships. And for the next few decades, they passed off the job of policing their coast to warships from nearby Greek cities that were already subjects of Rome.

Roman war galleys like these only occasionally fought in large sea battles. More often they ferried troops from one place to another, guarded ports and commercial ships, and chased after pirates.

Then came Rome's declaration of war against Carthage in 264 B.C. At first, the landlubbing Romans tried to defeat the enemy on the island of Sicily, the western half of which Carthage controlled. But these efforts were largely unsuccessful, as the Carthaginian navy kept its Sicilian strongholds well supplied. It was not long before Roman leaders accepted the hard reality that they would have to fight the Carthaginians on their own terms. Rome needed to seize control of the western Mediterranean sea lanes from the enemy. And to do so, it would have to construct a large fleet of warships.

This was an enormously tall order. The Romans had faint notions at best about how to build large, effective warships; they also lacked the thousands of specially trained crewmen required to operate the new fleet. Fortune seems to have been smiling on them in their hour of need, however, for they had recently come into possession of a Carthaginian warship that had accidentally run aground. "It was this ship which they proceeded to use as a model," Polybius wrote,

and they built their whole fleet according to its specifications; for which it is clear that but for this accident they would have been prevented from carrying out their program for sheer lack of necessary knowledge. As it was, those who had been given the task of shipbuilding occupied themselves with the construction work, while others collected the crews and began to teach them to row on shore in the

Carthage was long the preeminent naval power of the western Mediterranean. The Romans used a Carthaginian warship like the ones seen here as a model for their own war vessels.

AN ANCIENT DESCRIPTION OF THE "RAVEN"

In his Histories, *Polybius provides this detailed description of the* corvus, *the offensive naval device introduced by the Romans during the First Punic War.*

[The "raven"] was constructed as follows. A round pole about twenty-four feet high and ten inches in diameter was erected on the prow of the ship. At the top of this pole was a pulley, and at its base a gangway four feet in width and thirty-six in length made of planks which were nailed across each other. Twelve feet from one end of the gangway, an oblong slot was cut, into which the base of the pole was fitted, and each of the long sides of the gangway was protected by a rail as high as a man's knee. At the outboard [far] end of the gangway was fastened an iron spike. . . . When the ship charged an opponent, the "raven" would be hauled up by means of the pulley and then dropped onto the deck of the enemy vessel; this could either be done over the bows, or the gangway could be swiveled round if the two ships collided broadside on.

following way. They placed the men along the rowers' benches on dry land, seating them in the same order as if they were on those of an actual vessel, and then . . . trained them to swing back their bodies in unison. . . . When the crews had learned this drill, the ships were launched as soon as they were finished.[31]

Using this crash program of construction and training, Rome produced about 330 fully manned warships by 256 B.C. Though large numbers of these vessels were destroyed in battle or in violent storms, the Romans continually built new ships and fleets. In the course of the war, which was fought mostly at sea, they lost an estimated seven hundred warships and troop transports and over 100,000 crewmen (the largest naval losses ever suffered by a single nation in one war). Yet in their usual display of guts, determination, and

resiliency, they managed to win the war. They went on to vanquish the Carthaginians again in the Second Punic War; and by 201 B.C., at the conclusion of that conflict, Rome, which a mere seventy years before had possessed no war fleets at all, was the greatest sea power in the Mediterranean sphere.

As time went on, however, the size and strength of Rome's naval forces varied considerably as the government funded or neglected them according to changing circumstances. Once Carthage's war fleets had been eliminated, the only other navies that posed any threat to Rome's fleet were those of a few Greek states in the eastern Mediterranean. But by the mid–second century B.C., the Romans were in full control of this region; and with the sea lanes largely at peace, they allowed their navy to decline. Not until the civil wars of the late first century B.C. did the Romans require fleets of warships again. This time they acquired most of them from Greek cities under their control.

Following the civil wars, these ships became the nucleus of the imperial fleets organized by Augustus. In the early Empire, he and his successors established fleets of varying sizes on the coasts of Italy, Egypt, Syria, the Black Sea, the English Channel, and the Rhine and Danube Rivers. By the second century, however, with the known world largely at peace during the *Pax Romana*, these fleets began to decline. In the Empire's last few centuries, sea power played almost no role in warfare. And by the end of the fourth century, the once impressive Roman navy had virtually ceased to exist.

Types and Sizes of Roman Warships

During the periods when Rome's war fleets were well maintained and saw service, they consisted of a fairly wide variety of vessels. For the most part, though, the Romans mainly used four kinds of warships—triremes ("threes"), quadriremes ("fours"), quinqueremes ("fives"), and Liburnians. The original designs of the first three types were Greek. And over time a large proportion of the sailors who manned the Roman versions continued to be Greeks; if they lived long enough, these men gained Roman citizenship at the ends of their hitches.

As its name suggests, the trireme had three banks of oars, with one man to an

A large Roman warship with several rowers working each oar struggles in rough seas. The vessel's crowded decks show that it is transporting troops, most or all of whom will fight on land.

This relief sculpture found at Praeneste, southeast of Rome, shows a large war galley of the first century B.C. Many historians think it was carved to commemorate Octavian's victory at Actium.

oar. A Roman trireme probably carried a complement of about 220 to 250 men, including about 170 rowers (with between 50 and 60 men in each oar bank), about 15 to 20 crewmen, and a few dozen marines (fighters). Adding together the hull, decks, mast, oars, men, weapons, and supplies, such a vessel would have weighed, or in nautical terms "displaced," eighty to ninety tons. Yet it was relatively quick for its time. In short spurts, when attacking, for example, it could attain a speed of perhaps seven to eight knots (eight to nine miles per hour).

Two other common warships, the quadrireme and quinquereme, were both somewhat larger than a trireme. A quadrireme appears to have had two banks of oars, with two men to each oar. As for the quinquereme, modern scholars have long debated the numbers of its oar banks and rowers. However, most scholars have come to believe that such a vessel had three oar banks, with two men to an oar in each of the upper two banks and one man to an oar in the lower bank. Perhaps the most common warship in Roman navies during the mid to late Republic, the quinquereme was up to 120 feet long and carried some 270 rowers, 30 crewmen, and from 40 to 120 marines.

Much smaller than the trireme, quadrireme, or quinquereme was the Liburnian, invented by a tribe of pirates who inhabited what is now Bosnia. In Casson's words, a Liburnian was light, fast, and highly maneuverable, making it

> ideal for pursuit of pirates or for quick communications. . . . The Romans found it useful enough to adopt as a standard [naval] unit, particularly for the provincial fleets which used such craft almost exclusively. Originally, it was most probably single-banked, but its borrowers developed a heavier version driven by two banks of oarsmen. . . . Its two banks were easier to handle than the three of the [trireme and quinquereme] and . . . its mast and sail . . . perhaps could be lowered under way for a fight without disturbing the rowers. The Liburnian became so popular in the Roman navy that the term eventually came to mean warship in general.[32]

The crews of these ships gave them names, just as sailors name their boats today. Roman sailors did not follow the modern custom of writing a ship's name on the side of its hull, however; instead, they placed a wooden figurehead or other carving prominently on the bow. Many ships were named after gods and goddesses, particularly those associated with the sea. Widely popular were Neptune, lord of the sea; Neptune's son, Triton; and Nereus, the "old man of the sea," a god thought to possess the gift of prophecy. Roman sailors were also partial to Isis, an Egyptian goddess who came to be widely worshiped across the Roman Empire. Other common names for Roman war-

ships included important abstract concepts, such as Justice, Liberty, Peace, and Piety.

Methods of Warfare at Sea

Today it may seem surprising that in any given era these ships and crews rarely, if ever, actually took part in a military campaign. This was because Rome was at peace more often than it was at war. Those sailors who did experience the horrors of naval warfare faced a high risk of injury or death, especially by drowning when their ships suffered major damage and sank.

As in the case of ship designs and various naval customs, the Romans adopted basic naval battle practices and tactics from the Greeks, Carthaginians, and other Mediterranean maritime peoples. One of the primary tactics was to ram an enemy vessel with a bronze-coated beak mounted on a ship's bow. The object was to open a hole in an enemy ship's side and thereby to sink it. Various tactics developed to outmaneuver opposing vessels and make it easier to ram them, among them the *periplus*, in which an attacking fleet tried to outflank an enemy fleet. If the attackers succeeded in enveloping the sides of the opposing fleet, they could ram the exposed sides of the outer ships in the enemy's line. Another common maneuver was the *diekplus*, described here by Casson:

> In battle, opponents generally faced each other in two long lines. The one carrying out the *diekplus* would at a given signal dash forward so suddenly and swiftly that his ships were able to row through the enemy's line before the latter was able

In this photo of models constructed for the 1959 film of Lew Wallace's novel Ben Hur, *one warship rams another. Ramming was one of the chief tactics of ancient naval warfare.*

to take countermeasures, wheel [around] when through [the line], and ram the unprotected quarters or sterns [of the enemy's ships]. It was a deadly maneuver, but it demanded the utmost in coordination, response to command, and cleanness of execution; only fast ships and finely trained crews, taught to work in unison, could carry it out successfully.[33]

In another naval battle tactic, a ship attacked an enemy vessel at an angle, shearing off most of its oars on one side and thereby rendering it helpless; a second attacker, stationed directly behind the first, then moved in for the killing ramming run.

Although the Romans sometimes used these maneuvers, they much preferred the second basic naval battle tactic—boarding an enemy ship and taking control of it via hand-to-hand fighting. Perhaps it was the long and prestigious record of their land army that led to their increased emphasis of land warfare techniques in naval battles. The first major advance in this direction was their invention of the *corvus* ("crow" or "raven") in the early years of the First Punic War. This was a long wooden gangway with a spike attached to its end. The crow stood in an upright position on the front deck of a Roman ship until the vessel pulled up alongside an enemy ship, at which time sailors dropped the device onto the enemy's deck. The

ROME'S VICTORY AT CAPE ECNOMUS

What may have been the largest sea battle fought in ancient times took place in 256 B.C. at the height of the First Punic War. The Romans prepared to invade North Africa by sending some 330 warships, carrying some 140,000 sailors and marines, to Cape Ecnomus, on Sicily's southern shore. The Carthaginians countered this move by hurriedly assembling about 350 ships about forty miles west of the Roman fleet. In his *Histories*, the Greek historian Polybius describes the subsequent battle. He says that the Romans arranged their front ships in a wedge formation and smashed through the Carthaginian center. The Carthaginian ships were faster than the Roman ones, but the former were reluctant to come too close to the latter, which were equipped with "ravens," which the Romans used to hold fast and board enemy vessels. Eventually, the Romans gained the upper hand and their opponents fled. Over thirty Carthaginian ships were destroyed and another sixty or so were captured, while the Romans lost twenty-four ships. The Roman victory left the African coast vulnerable to attack, allowing Rome to carry the war to the Carthaginian homeland.

This photo from a 1937 Italian film shows a Roman warship outfitted with a "raven."

spike pierced the deck, holding the gangway in place, and Roman marines charged across and attacked the enemy vessel's crew. In republican times these marines were not sailors, but army legionaries who had been trained to adapt their use of *pilum*, sword, and shield to the narrow confines of ships' decks. Therefore, the *corvus*, Peter Connolly writes, "turned a naval battle into a fight between marines, which the superb Roman infantry were bound to win."[34]

Later, the Roman navy discontinued use of the *corvus* because its weight made their ships unbalanced, unsteady, and more prone to capsizing in stormy conditions. However, they continued to develop and use devices that allowed them to hold fast and board enemy ships. These included long poles or lengths of chain with large grapnels (hooks) attached to the ends; when their ship maneuvered close enough to an enemy vessel, Roman sailors tossed the grapnel, snagging the enemy's deck, and the marines boarded on wooden planks or ladders.

A more advanced version of these devices was introduced in the 30s B.C. by Augustus's talented admiral, Agrippa. Called the *harpax*, it was a grapnel with long ropes or chains attached. Specially trained marines shot it from a catapult mounted on the deck of a Roman ship, allowing an enemy ship to be ensnared from a much greater distance. Larger ships also sometimes featured wooden towers mounted on the deck at front and back; javelin men or archers stationed atop these towers fired down on an enemy ship's deck as the opposing ships neared each other, softening up the enemy before the marines boarded.

Officers and Crewmen

Fighting in such battles required a wide range of duties and skills, including rowing, steering, lowering the sails, and fighting, as well as commanding and coordinating offense and defense. So the breakdown of naval leaders and personnel was nearly as diverse as that of Rome's land forces. A man in the topmost naval position—admiral— was always a Roman citizen from a prominent family; noncitizens in the lower ranks could not aspire to his post. In the Republic the admirals, who commanded whole fleets and the home bases where these fleets docked, were usually senators. Imperial admirals, in contrast, held the rank of prefect and tended to be well-to-do, high-ranking army officers. (That these admirals came from the army rather than the navy reflected and reinforced the common perception that the navy was the inferior of the two services.)

The Romans borrowed the terms used to describe most of the other naval officers from the Greeks. The commander of a squadron, perhaps about ten ships, was a *navarch* (from the Greek *navarchos*); and the captain of an individual ship was called a *trierarch* (from the Greek *trierarchos*). *Navarchs* were generally promoted from the position of *trierarch*, and *trierarchs* were likely promoted from the lower ranks of navy men. In the early Empire, both positions were filled mainly by experienced Greek sailors.

Just as several junior officers existed under an army tribune, a naval captain had his own staff of junior officers. These included a chief administrator and various kinds of clerks with specialized jobs, such

RIDDING THE SEA LANES OF PIRATES

One important way the Romans used warships was to chase down and destroy pirate vessels. The most spectacular instance occurred in the first century B.C. By the third decade of that century, piracy had become so bad that bands of brigands had started coming ashore on Italy's western coast, where they robbed and burned houses and mugged or kidnapped travelers on Roman roads. Pirate ships also sank a small group of Roman warships and in 69 B.C. sacked the Greek island of Delos (an important marketing center), crippling Mediterranean shipping. That was the last straw for the Romans. In 67 B.C. they assigned the popular general Pompey the task of ridding the sea lanes of the pirate menace. In an unprecedented move, the government gave him supreme (though temporary) command of the Mediterranean Sea and all of its coasts to a distance of fifty miles inland. In a lightning campaign of only forty days, he literally swept the sea of pirates, destroying their strongholds and sinking or capturing over seventeen hundred of their vessels, all without the loss of a single Roman ship! Needless to say, this incredible achievement virtually eliminated the danger of pirates, while making Pompey a hero of epic proportions.

as making reports to the admiral's office and keeping financial records. The *trierarch* also had deck officers to help him run his ship. Among them were the *gubernator* (the term from which the word "governor" evolved), who supervised the steersmen from his station on the aft (rear) deck; his assistant, stationed on the prow (front), who kept an eye out for rocks and shoals in the vessel's path; a man who used wooden mallets to pound out a beat for the rowers to follow; two or three experts at raising and lowering the sails; and a *nauphlax*, who had charge of the ship's physical upkeep. (It is probable that only larger ships, like quinqueremes, had a full complement of such specialists; the fewer crewmen manning Liburnians and other small craft likely doubled up on these jobs.) Usually, these junior officers and specialists received double or more the pay of an ordinary sailor.

Each warship also had its complement of marines. Since for organizational purposes an individual warship was designated as a naval century, these fighters were trained and commanded by a centurion. As in an army century, he was assisted by an *optio*. The relationship between the centurion and the *trierarch*, including who had more authority in specific areas, remains unclear. But it is almost certain that the centurion made all the important decisions concerning actual combat.

Finally came the lowest-ranking naval personnel—the rowers and other ordinary sailors. They were well aware of the drawbacks of naval service when they signed up. Besides the navy's secondary status as a service branch, they faced long hitches featuring hard and sometimes dangerous work and little pay. Still, for a poor boy from an Italian or provincial farm or city slum, the rewards of serving in the navy could well outweigh the drawbacks. Even if small, the pay was steady and often amounted to more than he could make as a farmhand or ordinary laborer. There was also the opportunity for travel and seeing faraway cities and peoples. And most important of all were the possibilities of promotion and eventually becoming a citizen. These potential benefits motivated and sustained the crews of thousands ships during the centuries that Roman warfare shaped and reshaped the Mediterranean world.

The Decline and Fall of Rome's Military

The renowned decline and fall of the Roman Empire did not happen suddenly or quickly. It was a gradual process that happened in fits and starts, with various and diverse causes, over the course of almost three centuries. Moreover, both mirroring and significantly contributing to the Empire's decline was the decline of the Roman military. Warfare and the armed forces required to wage it effectively had made Rome strong and long maintained the integrity of its realm; so it is not surprising that when the Romans could no longer wage war effectively, that realm fell apart.

CHAPTER SIX

From Order to Near Anarchy

The story of the decline of the Empire and its military establishment begins at the close of the period when these entities were at their height—the *Pax Romana* ("Roman Peace," ca. 30 B.C. to A.D. 180). Rome was enormously, strong, ordered, stable, and prosperous in this era mainly because Augustus and most of his immediate succes-

sors were thoughtful, effective rulers. The five emperors who ruled from 96 to 180—Nerva, Trajan, Hadrian, Antoninus Pius, and Marcus Aurelius—were especially capable and enlightened leaders, hence the name posterity accorded then—the "five good emperors." They brought Roman civilization to its political, economic, and cultural zenith.

Indeed, under the second good emperor, Trajan, an able, thoughtful, and generous ruler, the Empire was larger than it had ever been or ever would be. It stretched from the Atlantic Ocean in the west to the Persian Gulf in the east, and from north Africa in the south to central Britain in the north. The huge realm covered some 3.5 million square miles and supported over 100 million inhabitants.

Those inhabitants could not have predicted that the death of the fifth good emperor, Marcus Aurelius, in 180, would mark the end of the largely safe and happy *Pax Romana*. Thereafter, the Empire's political and economic problems rapidly increased, leading to a century of severe crisis in which the Roman realm approached the brink of total collapse. The crisis had several dimensions and causes, among them poor leadership, as one ambitious, brutal, and/or incompetent individual after another occupied the throne; and serious economic problems, including a shortage of precious metals, rising inflation, and declining agriculture.

Worst of all, the Empire faced grave military threats, as large semi-nomadic Germanic tribes assaulted its northern borders. At the same time, the Roman army, though larger than ever, had by the early third century grown less disciplined and reliable than it had been in the past; so it was often unable to stop enemy incursions into Roman territory. Making mat-

ters worse, army units in various parts of the realm swore allegiance to their generals, much as in late republican times, and these leaders frequently and foolishly tried to fight one another while defending against the invaders. During the ensuing roughly fifty-year period of near anarchy, more than fifty rulers claimed the throne. And all but one of them died by assassination or other violent means.

Chaos, disunity, and invasions threatened to tear the Roman world asunder. Yet Rome managed, seemingly miraculously, to pull back from the brink of ruin. Beginning in the year 268, a series of strong military leaders took control, and in the next sixteen years they both pushed back the Germans and defeated illegal imperial claimants in various parts of the realm.

Trajan, one of the five "good" emperors, dominates this sculpted scene from his famous column in Rome. He appears sixty times in all, always slightly larger than the other figures.

With the Empire reunited and minimal order restored, in 284 a very intelligent and capable leader named Diocletian ascended the throne. He initiated numerous reforms—substantially reorganizing the provinces, the tax system, and the imperial court—creating what was in effect a new Roman Empire. Modern historians often refer to this realm, a grimmer, more dangerous and regimented, and far less optimistic society than that of the *Pax Romana* era, as the Later Empire.

A New Round of Military Reforms

One of Diocletian's most important and far-reaching reforms, which his immediate suc-

cessors continued, was a thorough overhaul of the military. The new army that emerged reflected a general change in the Empire's overall strategic approach to warfare, one that had been developing for some time and would ultimately lead to weakness and disaster. Put simply, the Roman military, which had for so many centuries operated offensively, went on the defense.

Shaping this new outlook was the sober reality of many decades of relentless barbarian incursions across the northern frontiers. Roman leaders now accepted the idea that it was no longer possible to make the borders (*limes*) completely impregnable; some invaders, the reasoning went, must be expected to get through the line of forts along the frontiers. However, these intruders could hopefully be intercepted by one or more small, swiftly moving mobile armies stationed at key points in the border provinces. To make such "defense-in-depth" strategy work, historian Arther Ferrill points out, the forts had to be "strong enough to withstand attack and yet not so strongly defended as to become a drain on manpower, weakening the mobile army."[35]

A step in the direction of less static defenses had been taken in the 260s by the emperor Gallienus (reigned 253–268), who recruited extra cavalry forces for a mobile army that could move independently of the slow-moving main legions. Diocletian now took the idea a step further. He stationed small armies, each accompanied by detachments of cavalry, at key positions on the frontiers. He also attached two highly trained legions to his personal traveling court, the *comitatus*, supported by elite cavalry forces, the *scholae*, thus creating a fast and very effective mobile field force.

One of Diocletian's immediate successors, Constantine I (reigned 307–337), further elaborated on these changes. Like Diocletian, he divided his military into both mobile forces, the *comitatenses* (from *comitatus*), and frontier troops, the *limitanei* (from *limes*). However, Constantine withdrew troops from some frontier forts and used them to create several small mobile armies. These patrolled the frontiers, traveling from town to town; when needed, they hurried to any new trouble spots.[36]

The actual size of these armies, as well as of Rome's overall forces in the Later Empire, is difficult to calculate and often disputed. A realistic figure for the Empire's combined armies in the first half of

SUPREME COMMANDERS IN THE LATER EMPIRE

The titles of Rome's supreme military leaders in the Later Empire grew out of terms coined in earlier centuries. For example, in the Republic, the *magister equitum* ("master of the horse") was the principal assistant and deputy of the dictator (on those rare occasions when the state appointed a dictator). Augustus eliminated the position of master of the horse; but in the Later Empire, Constantine I decided to revive the title. This time it referred to the leading general of Rome's cavalry, while the leader of the infantry was the *magister peditum*. Soon their titles and duties merged into one overall military leader—the *magister militum* ("master of soldiers"). In the western Empire's last century, the *magistri* often came to dominate not only military affairs, but also their supposed masters, the emperors. This was because Roman troops, who were increasingly Germanic or otherwise foreign in character, tended to show more allegiance to their generals (who were often of "barbarian" extraction themselves) than to the government. And these powerful generals frequently made decisions on their own that were not in the best interests of the already deteriorating western Roman state.

the fourth century is perhaps 400,000. At first glance this sounds truly formidable. But it turns out to be much less so after certain realistic limitations are factored in. First, army lists were frequently inflated with fictitious entries, such as the names of little boys and old men attempting to draw free pay and rations. There were also high desertion rates, spotty training, and inadequate supplies (caused in large part because of the government's shortage of funds).

Finally, and as it turned out very significantly, the military was composed of numerous small forces dispersed across a huge realm, the individual field armies being tiny in comparison to those of republican times. Each of Constantine's mobile army units likely consisted of little more than a thousand infantry and five hundred cavalry. These were sometimes combined to form larger armies, of course; but only rarely did generals in the Later Empire field forces numbering in the tens of thousands.

Adrianople: A Crucial Military Turning Point

The Empire's new overall military strategy of relying on frontier forts and small mobile armies worked well enough as long as barbarian incursions in the north were infrequent and fairly small scale. As time went on, however, these invasions became both more numerous and much larger in size. About 370 a fierce nomadic people from

The emperor Gallienus (left) conceived the idea of a quick-moving mobile army; his successor Diocletian (right) built on this concept, as did the emperor Constantine I.

A nineteenth-century engraving depicts the fearsome Huns on the move. A contemporary description of the Huns calls them "two-legged animals" who practically lived on horseback.

central Asia—the infamous Huns—swept into eastern Europe, forcing the Goths, Vandals, Franks, Alani, and other European tribes (whom the Romans called barbarians) to flee and search for new lands. The following graphic description of the Huns by the fourth-century Roman historian Ammianus Marcellinus explains why they ap-

peared repulsive and frightening even to the Germanic barbarians.

[The Huns] are quite abnormally savage. . . . They have squat bodies, strong limbs, and thick necks, and are so prodigiously ugly and bent that they might be two-legged

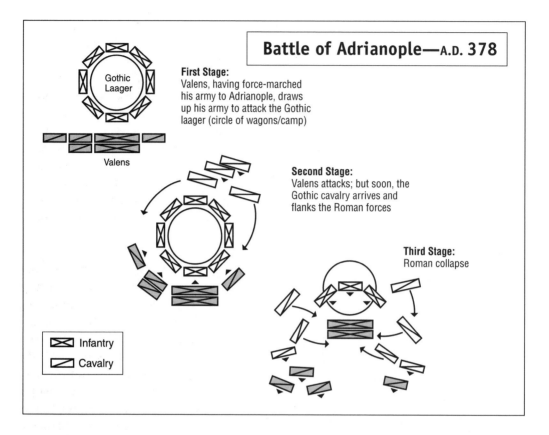

Battle of Adrianople—A.D. 378

Gothic Laager

First Stage:
Valens, having force-marched his army to Adrianople, draws up his army to attack the Gothic laager (circle of wagons/camp)

Valens

Second Stage:
Valens attacks; but soon, the Gothic cavalry arrives and flanks the Roman forces

Third Stage:
Roman collapse

Infantry
Cavalry

animals. . . . Their way of life is so rough that they have no use for fire or seasoned food, but live on the roots of wild plants and the half-raw flesh of any sort of animals, which they warm a little by placing it between their thighs and the backs of their horses. . . . Once they have put their necks into some dingy shirt they never take it off or change it till it rots and falls to pieces. . . . When they join battle they advance in packs, uttering their various war-cries. Being lightly equipped and very sudden in their movements they can deliberately scatter and gallop about at random, inflicting tremendous slaughter.[37]

As the uprooted Goths and other groups pressed on and entered some of Rome's northern border provinces, the Roman army was by now inadequate to the task of keeping all the intruders out. This became most painfully clear on August 9, 378, a date that now joined those of Allia and Cannae in the annals of humiliating Roman military defeats. The emperor Valens (reigned 364–378) attempted to halt the advance of some 200,000 members of a branch of the Goths, the Visigoths, who had earlier poured across the Danube River. The opposing armies met near Adrianople, in northern Greece; there, Valens suffered utter defeat and died along with at least two-thirds of his army, perhaps as many as forty thousand men. As Ammianus described the fateful encounter:

> Amid the clashing of arms and weapons on every side . . . sounding the death-knell of the Roman cause, our retreating troops rallied with shouts of mutual encouragement. But, as the fighting spread like fire and numbers of them were transfixed by arrows and whirling javelins, they lost heart. Then the opposing lines came into collision like ships of war and pushed each other to and fro, heaving under the reciprocal motion like the waves of the sea. Our left wing . . . gave way and collapsed like a broken dike. This left the infantry unprotected and so closely huddled together that a man could hardly wield his sword or draw back his arm once he had stretched it out. Dust rose in such clouds as to hide the sky, which rang with frightful shouts. . . . The barbarians poured on in huge columns, trampling down horse and man and crushing our ranks so as to make an orderly retreat impossible. . . . In this mutual slaughter so many were laid low that the field was covered with the bodies of the slain, while the groans of the dying and severely wounded filled all who heard them with abject fear.[38]

When news of the catastrophe reached Italy, Ambrose, a leading Christian bishop, called it "the massacre of all humanity, the end of the world."[39] Ambrose had exaggerated, for this one defeat, though crippling, was not enough to bring down the Empire. Yet his words bore an element of truth. In a way the disaster at Adrianople marked a crucial turning point for Rome, the beginning of a military-political downward spiral that would eventually seal its fate. Thereafter, the barbarian invasions

SCHOLARS AIDED BY THE *NOTITIA DIGNITATUM*

Very little contemporary written evidence about the military in Rome's last two centuries has survived. One notable exception is the *Notitia Dignitatum*, a list of political and military officials and their staffs that provides some information about the duties and military units of each. It was compiled by an unknown person or persons some time around A.D. 400 or perhaps a bit later. Regrettably, most of the information concerns officials in the western part of the realm rather the whole Empire, and the work does not list all of Rome's garrisons, forts, and military units. Still, modern scholars find the *Notitia* an invaluable aid in understanding how the deteriorating late Roman government and army worked.

A RESILIENT ENEMY: THE VANDALS

The Vandals were one of the most resilient and successful of the Germanic tribes who threatened the Later Empire. Their original homeland appears to have been northern Germany, near the Baltic Sea, but by the mid-second century A.D., they had migrated southward to the region now occupied by Hungary. In the years to come, they periodically raided Roman border provinces. But they posed a much bigger threat beginning in the early fifth century when they joined other Germans in crossing the Rhine River into Gaul. Soon, feeling pressure from other barbarian groups entering Gaul, the Vandals moved farther south into Spain. They began to settle there, but in 416 the Visigoths invaded the area and attacked them. About three years later, the Vandals decided that they must find still another new home. They built a fleet of ships and landed in the Balearic Islands (off Spain's eastern coast). Then, in 429, led by an ambitious and capable man named Gaiseric, they landed in Africa. His forces swept eastward, overrunning the region's Roman provinces; and soon Gaiseric established a new and powerful Vandal kingdom, with its capital at Carthage. Not satisfied with these gains, in 455 the Vandals sailed north to Italy's western coast, sacked Rome, and also terrorized the coasts of Sicily, Sardinia, and Corsica. The Vandal kingdom survived the western Empire's fall (in 476) and prospered until the 530s, when an expedition sent by the eastern emperor Justinian destroyed it.

continued to *in*crease, while the quality and morale of the Roman army steadily *de*creased.

The Barbarization of the Military

One major reason for the continued decline of the Roman military was that by the end of the fourth century many of its members were barbarians themselves. This process of so-called "barbarization" had begun in prior centuries when the government had allowed Germans from the northern frontier areas to settle in Roman lands. Once these settlers had established themselves, they were more than willing to fight Rome's enemies, including fellow Germans; and Roman leaders, always in need of tough military recruits, took advantage of that fact. However, as the recruitment of Germans into the military accelerated, this policy began to take its toll, particularly in a loss of discipline, traditionally one of the Roman army's greatest strengths. According to Ferrill, the German recruits

> began immediately to demand great rewards for their service and to show an independence that in drill, discipline and organization meant catastrophe. They fought under their own native commanders, and the barbaric system of discipline was in no way as severe as the Roman. Eventually Roman soldiers saw no reason to do what barbarian troops in Roman service were rewarded heavily for not doing. . . . Too long

and too close association with barbarian warriors, as allies in the Roman army, had ruined the qualities that made Roman armies great. . . . The Roman army of A.D. 440, in the west, had become little more than a barbarian army itself.[40]

More than two centuries of barbarization and other aspects of military evolution also brought about significant changes in armor. Most Roman body armor in the Later Empire was either the old-style iron-ringed mail or scale armor, consisting of rows of small, thin bronze or iron scales attached to a linen or leather tunic. (The more expensive *lorica segmentata* had been abandoned by the mid–third century.) But the passage of time witnessed a reduced use even of mail and scale armor, as some

This infantryman of a Roman comitatenses *protects his torso with the scale armor that was common in the Later Empire.*

soldiers wore whatever they could afford to buy or scrape together and others wore no armor at all. One reason was that the government was increasingly impoverished and could not afford to supply all soldiers with standardized equipment; another was that the Germans, who increasingly filled the army ranks, often viewed such armor as cumbersome and unnecessary. According to Vegetius, who lived during the Empire's last decades: "It is plain that the infantry are completely exposed. . . . Negligence and sloth, having by degrees introduced a total relaxation of discipline, the soldiers began to consider their armor too heavy and seldom put it on."[41]

Weapons use and battle tactics also underwent change. Late Roman army weapons included a long sword worn on the left side; a javelin (now called the *spiculum* rather than the *pilum*); the bow and arrow; a throwing ax (introduced by the Franks and other Germans); and the *plumbata*, a lead-weighted dart about twenty inches long, of which a soldier carried five attached to the inside of his wooden shield.[42] As for battle

These modern reenactors display common weapons of late Roman infantry soldiers, including plumbatae *(darts), wielded by the man at left, and the* spiculum, *carried by the one at right.*

The Infantry Sword of the Later Empire

In this excerpt from The Late Roman Army, *Pat Southern and Karen Dixon, scholars at the University of Newcastle upon Tyne, describe the sword that replaced the traditional* gladius *for use by Roman infantrymen in the Later Empire.*

The long sword (*spatha*) was the dominant form employed by the Roman army from the late second/early third century onwards. . . . The sword [with a blade typically about twenty-seven inches long] was now carried on a baldric [a long belt worn over one shoulder] and worn on the left side, rather than the right [as the *gladius* had been. Eventually, the baldric was replaced by a belt worn around the hips]. The blades could be [forged and] decorated in various ways. [For example,] pattern-welding was a process which involved forged strands of iron and steel being twisted and welded together. . . . The cutting edges were then welded on to the core, and the whole blade was filed down [to the desired shape and sharpness].

tactics, the emphasis on smaller armies and the influence of less-disciplined German battlefield organization caused the traditional, highly organized system of cohorts and manipular tactics to disappear. The infantry fought in a phalanx-like mass of troops, though it was not as tightly organized and well-trained as an old-style phalanx. In battle, two such masses crashed together. As the front ranks of one army tried to shove back their opponents and strike at them with their swords, men in the rear ranks rained volleys of arrows, javelins, darts, and axes onto the enemy rear ranks; meanwhile, cavalry units tried to attack the sides and/or rear of the enemy formation.

The End of the Army and the Realm

Other problems besides barbarization contributed to the decline of the military. First, as financial problems increasingly beset both imperial and town government, as well as families and individuals, the tasks and duties of the average Roman soldier became increasingly thankless and hopeless. The soldiers were not only paid very little, but because of the government's frequent lack of money, their wages were often months or even years in arrears, which severely damaged morale. Serving in the military, once a prestigious and coveted goal, steadily lost its allure.

Because fewer Roman men enlisted in the army than had in prior, more peaceful times, the government resorted to making service compulsory for the sons of veterans and eventually for many others. But conscription remained unpopular and difficult to enforce. To avoid serving, some young men resorted to extreme measures, such as amputating their own thumbs. "Those who tried to evade their duty were liable to be rounded up by recruiting officers," historian Stewart Perowne explains.

Every estate or village, or group of villages, had to provide so many re-

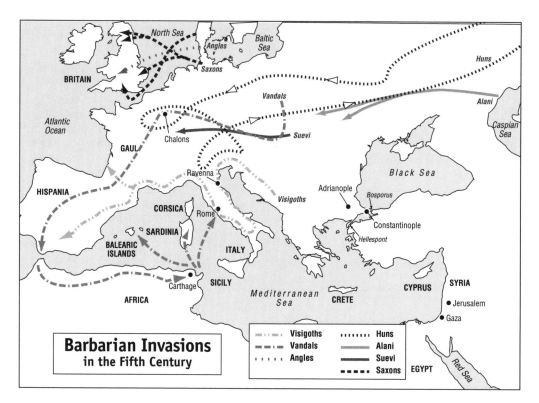

Barbarian Invasions
in the Fifth Century

cruits every so many years. The levy fell wholly on the rural population. . . . As soon as they were enrolled, recruits were branded, as a precaution against desertion. This fact alone shows how unpopular the service had become, and consequently how hard it now was to find enough recruits.[43]

Adding to the increasing shortage of manpower was a side effect of Christianity after it became the official state religion in the fourth century. Increasing numbers of Christians refused to fight, claiming it violated their moral principles.

As these problems grew worse and took their toll over time, the traditional Roman soldier and army—highly disci-

plined, well organized and trained, tough and tenacious, eager and willing to defend both family and the Roman state—steadily deteriorated. The ongoing military decline, coupled with the continuing invasions and severe economic decay, caused the western Roman Empire to shrink drastically in size and power. (The eastern portion of the Empire, centered at Constantinople, in what is now northern Turkey, escaped most of the invasions and remained largely intact; in time, it mutated into the Greek-speaking Byzantine Empire.) The last few western emperors ruled over a pitiful realm consisting only of the Italian peninsula and portions of a few nearby provinces.

Even these lands were not safe or secure, for claims by German tribes on Roman territory continued. In 476 a German-born general named Odoacer, who commanded the last of all the Roman armies in Italy, demanded that he and his soldiers be granted lands in which to settle. When the government refused, Odoacer's men acclaimed him king of Italy. And on September 4, he deposed the young emperor Romulus Augustulus in a bloodless coup. No new emperor took the boy's place, and most later scholars came to view the event as the fall of the western Empire.

As for the western Roman army, except for a few regiments of Germans in Italy, it had already disintegrated, forever ending the long saga of Roman warfare. Scholars Pat Southern and Karen Dixon describe one haunting example of the often silent, insidious process:

> While the Romans were in power, soldiers were maintained in many towns at public expense to guard the frontier. But when this custom ceased, several whole units of soldiers disappeared. The men at Batava [on the Danube frontier] remained at their posts, and sent a delegation to Italy to find out why they had received no pay. Some days later their bodies floated down-river and came to rest on the banks, silent testimony to the end of Rome's ability to keep her Empire intact and to defend her frontiers.[44]

Legions of the
Early Empire

Notes: *Legion*: name of legion. *Formed/Raised by*: year recruited and by whom. *Cognomina:* what the legion's title means. *Emblem:* the legion's symbol. A ? indicates incomplete or unknown data.

Legion	Formed/ Raised by	Cognomina	Emblem	Notes
I Adiutrix	68 A.D./Nero	"Supportive"	Trireme	Recruited from sailors
I Germanica	48 B.C.?/Caesar	"Service in Germania"	?	Disbanded 69 A.D., revolt of Civilis
I Italica	66/67 A.D./Nero	"Recruited from Italians"	?	
I Minervia	83 A.D./Domitian	"Sacred to Minerva"	Minerva	
I Parthica	197 A.D./Severus	"Service in Parthia"	Dragon	Raised for Severus's Parthian War
II Adiutrix	69 A.D./Vespasian	"Supportive"	Trireme	Recruited from sailors
II Augusta	43 B.C.?/ Augustus	After Augustus	Capricorn	Also called II Gallica and II Sabina
II Italica	165 A.D./ M. Aurelius	"Recruited from Italians"	?	Raised for Marcomanic War
II Parthica	197 A.D./Severus	"Service in Parthia"	Dragon	Stationed near Rome after Civil War of A.D. 194–197
II Traiana Fortis	101 A.D./Trajan	Raised by Trajan/"Strong"	?	Raised for Dacian Wars
III Augusta	43 B.C.?/ Augustus	After Augustus	Pegasus	
III Cyrenaica	30 B.C.?/ Augustus	Service in North Africa	?	
III Gallica	48 B.C.?/Caesar	"Service in Gaul"	Bull	
III Italica Concors	168 A.D./ M. Aurelius	"Recruited from Italians"	?	
III Parthica	197 A.D./Severus	"Service in Parthia"	Dragon	Raised for Severus's Parthian War

102

Legion	Formed/ Raised by	Cognomina	Emblem	Notes
IV Macedonica	48 B.C./?	"Service in Macedonia"	Bull, Capricorn	Reconstituted as IV Flavia Felix, 70 A.D.
IV Flavia Firma	70 A.D./ Vespasian	"Steadfast to Flavians"	?	
IV Scythica	30 B.C.?/ Augustus	"For victories over Scythians"	Capricorn	Disbanded 68 A.D., revolt of Civilis
V Alaudae	52 B.C./Caesar	Celtic for "The Larks"	Elephant	Destroyed/disbanded 86 A.D.?
V Macedonica	43 B.C./Caesar	"Service in Macedonia"	Bull	Longest continually existing military unit in history (43 B.C.–650 A.D.)
VI Ferrata	52 B.C./Caesar	"Ironclad," indicates endurance	(Gemini) Wolf, Twins	
VI Victrix	41–40 B.C./Caesar	"Victorious"	Bull	Also titled VI Hispaniensis
VII Claudia Pia Fidelis	59 B.C.?/Caesar	"Loyalty to Emperor Claudius"	Bull	
VII Gemina	70 A.D.?/Galba	"Twin"	Gemini	Two legions from one
VII Hispania	68 A.D./Nero	"Of Hispania"	?	Split to form VII Gemina
VIII Augusta	59 B.C.?/Caesar	Commemorating Augustus's victory in Spain	Bull	Originally titled Gallica, Mutinensis
IX Hispania	?/Caesar	"Of Hispania"	?	Disbanded 2nd century A.D. (165 A.D.?)
X Fretensis	59 B.C./Caesar	"Of the Straits" (of Messena)	Bull, Trireme, Dolphin	Title refers to participation in amphibious operations
X Gemina	59 B.C./Caesar	"Twin"	Bull	Amalgamation of two legions
XI Claudia Pia Fidelis	?/Augustus	"Loyalty to Emperor Claudius"	Neptune	
XII Fulminata	58 B.C.?/Pompey?	"Lightning Hurler"	Eagle w/ thunderbolt	
XIII Gemina Pia Fidelis	?/Augustus	"Twin"	Lion	Amalgamation of two legions
XIV Gemina Martia Victrix	?/Augustus	"Twin"	Capricorn	Amalgamation of two legions "Martial and Victorious" for victory over Boudicca, 60 A.D.
XV Apollinaris	41/40 B.C./ Augustus	"Sacred to Apollo"	?	
XV Primigenia	39 A.D./Caligula	After goddess Fortuna Primigenia	?	Disbanded 70 A.D., revolt of Civilis
XVI Gallica	41–40 B.C./ Augustus	"Service in Gaul"		Reconstituted as XVI Flavia Firma in 70 A.D.
XVII Augustus	41–40 B.C./	?	?	Destroyed in 9 A.D. at Teuterburgerwald
XVIII Augustus	41–40 B.C./	?	?	Destroyed in 9 A.D. at Teuterburgerwald

Legion	Formed/ Raised by	Cognomina	Emblem	Notes
XIX	41–40 B.C./ Augustus	?	?	Destroyed in 9 A.D. at Teuterburgerwald
XX Valeria Victrix	41–40 B.C./ Augustus	"Valiant and Victorious"	Boar	Titled Victrix after defeat of Boudicca, 60 A.D.
XXI Rapax	41–40 B.C./ Augustus	"Grasping" (as a bird of prey)	Capricorn	Destroyed in the Dobruja under Domitian
XXII Deiotariana	25 B.C.?/ Deiotarus	Raised by Deiotarus, king of Galatia	?	Destroyed or disbanded 135 A.D.
XXII Primigenia	39 A.D./Caligula	After goddess Fortuna Primigenia	?	
XXX Ulpia Victrix	101 A.D./Trajan	After Marcus Ulpia Traianus	?	Title Victrix added after distinguished conduct in Dacian Wars
Praetorian Guard	27 B.C./ Augustus	After Praetors: early Republic magistrates	Scorpion	Disbanded by Constantine, 312 A.D.

Sources: Parker: *The Roman Legions;* Webster: *The Roman Imperial Army;* La Bohec: *The Imperial Roman Army.*

Distribution of the Legions A.D. 23 to 138

This table shows the increasing importance of the Danube River frontier as legions were strategically redeployed to the provinces of Pannonia and Moesia to meet the increasing barbarian threat. As a province became more Romanized it needed fewer legions.

Province	23 A.D.	68 A.D.	106 A.D.	138 A.D.
Germania Inferior	I Germanica V Alaudae XX Valeria XXI Rapax	I Germanica V Alaudae XV Primigenia XVI Gallica	I Minervia VI Victrix	I Minervia XXII Primigenia
Germania Superior	II Augusta XIII Gemina XIV Gemina XVI Gallica	IV Macedonica XXI Rapax XXII Primigenia	VIII Augusta XXII Primigenia	VIII Augusta XXX Ulpia Victrix
Dalmatia	XI Hispania VII Macedonica	XI Claudia Pia Fidelis		
Moesia	IV Scythica V Macedonica	III Gallica VII Claudia Pia FidelisVII	IV Flavia Felix Claudia Pia Fidelis XXX Ulpia Victrix II Triana I Italica V Macedonica XI Claudia Pia Fidelis	IV Flavia Firma VII Claudia P.F. I Italica V Macedonica XI Claudia P.F.
Pannonia	VIII Augusta IX Hispania XV Apollonaris	X Gemina XIII Gemina VIII Augusta	II Aduitrix X Gemina XIV Gemina XV Apollonaris	I Aduitrix P.F. II Aduitrix P.F. X Gemina XIV Gemina M.V.

Province	23 A.D.	68 A.D.	106 A.D.	138 A.D.
Syria lica		III Gallica	IV Scythia	III Gallica III Gal-
	VI Ferrata X Fretensis XII Fulminata	VI Ferrata X Fretensis	IV Scythica VI Ferrata	IV Scythica XVI Flavia Firma
Judea Fretensis			V Macedonica	X FretensisX
		XII Fulminata XV Apollonaris		VI Ferrata
Egypt	III Cyrenaica XXII Deiotariana	III Cyrenaica XXII Deiotariana	III Cyrenaica XXII Deiotariana	II Triana Fortis
Africa	III Augusta	III Augusta	III Augusta	III Augusta
Hispania	IV Macedonica VI Martia Victrix X Gemina	VI Martia Victrix	VII Gemina	VII Gemina
Italy Praetorian Guard		Praetorian Guard XIV Gemina Martia V.	Praetorian Guard	Praetorian Guard
Britain		II Augusta IX Hispania XX Valeria Victrix	II Augusta IX Hispania XX Valeria Victrix	II Augusta IX Hispania XX Valeria Victrix
Lugdunum (Imperial Mint)		I Italica		
Dacia			I Adiutrix Pia Fidelis XIII Gemina	XIII Gemina
Cappadocia			XII Fulminata XVI Flavia Firma	XII Fulminata XV Apollonaris
Arabia Peteria				III Cyrenaica
Total		**25**	**28**	**30** **29**

Notes

Introduction: Rome's Unique Approach to Warfare

1. Polybius, *The Histories*, trans. Ian Scott-Kilvert. New York: Penguin, 1979, p. 415.

2. Michael Grant, *History of Rome*. New York: Scribner's, 1978, pp. 65–66.

Chapter 1: The Early Roman Army

3. Peter Connolly, *Greece and Rome at War*. London: Macdonald, 1998, pp. 92–93.

4. John Warry, *Warfare in the Classical World*. Norman: University of Oklahoma Press, 1995, p. 37.

5. Quoted in Kenneth J. Atchity, ed., *The Classical Greek Reader*. New York: Oxford University Press, 1996, p. 43.

6. Livy, *The History of Rome from Its Foundation*. Books 1–5 published as *Livy: The Early History of Rome*, trans. Aubrey de Sélincourt. New York: Penguin, 1971, p. 81.

7. Lawrence Keppie, *The Making of the Roman Army: From Republic to Empire*. New York: Barnes and Noble, 1984, p. 14.

8. Livy, *History of Rome*, in *Livy: The Early History of Rome*, pp. 383–84.

Chapter 2: The Development of Manipular Tactics

9. Keppie, *Making of the Roman Army*, p. 19.

10. Polybius, *Histories*, p. 320.

11. Polybius, *Histories*, p. 321.

12. Connolly, *Greece and Rome at War*, p. 142.

13. Polybius, *Histories*, pp. 273–74.

14. Polybius, *Histories*, p. 509.

15. Keppie, *Making of the Roman Army*, p. 19.

16. Connolly, *Greece and Rome at War*, pp. 205–206.

Chapter 3: The Professional Imperial Military Forces

17. Plutarch, *Life of Marius* (part of the larger *Parallel Lives*), in *Fall of the Roman Republic: Six Lives by Plutarch*, trans. Rex Warner. New York: Penguin, 1972, p. 25.

18. Polybius, *Histories*, p. 513.

19. Vegetius, *On the Roman Military*, quoted in Michael Grant, *The Army of*

the Caesars. New York: M. Evans, 1974, p. xxvii.

20. Vegetius, *On the Roman Military*, quoted in G.R. Watson, *The Roman Soldier*. London: Thames and Hudson, 1969, p. 57.

21. Michael Simkins, *Warriors of Rome: An Illustrated History of the Roman Legions*. London: Blandford, 1988, pp. 22–23.

Chapter 4: Fortifications and Siege Warfare

22. Connolly, *Greece and Rome at War*, p. 274.

23. Aeneas Tacticus, *On the Defense of Fortified Positions*, quoted in Sidney Toy, *Castles: Their Construction and History*. New York: Dover, 1984, p. 17.

24. Brian Dobson, "The Empire," in Sir John Hackett, ed., *Warfare in the Ancient World*. New York: Facts On File, 1989, p. 218.

25. Graham Webster, *The Roman Imperial Army*. Totowa, NJ: Barnes and Noble, 1985, p. 204.

26. Connolly, *Greece and Rome at War*, pp. 292–93.

27. Caesar, *Commentaries on the Gallic Wars*, in *War Commentaries of Caesar*, trans. Rex Warner. New York: New American Library, 1960, pp. 172–73.

Chapter 5: Naval Weapons and Tactics

28. Polybius, *Histories*, p. 62.

29. Lionel Casson, *The Ancient Mariners:*

Seafarers and Sea Fighters of the Mediterranean in Ancient Times. Princeton, NJ: Princeton University Press, 1991, p. 157.

30. Quoted in Casson, *Ancient Mariners*, p. 211.

31. Polybius, *Histories*, p. 63.

32. Casson, *Ancient Mariners*, pp. 213–14.

33. Casson, *Ancient Mariners*, p. 101.

34. Connolly, *Greece and Rome at War*, p. 273.

Chapter 6: The Decline and Fall of Rome's Military

35. Arther Ferrill, *The Fall of the Roman Empire: The Military Explanation*. New York: Thames and Hudson, 1986, p. 45.

36. The exact nature and chronology of Rome's frontier forts and mobile armies is still a matter of debate among historians. Some argue that the existence of a defense-in-depth strategy is uncertain because archaeological evidence for it is scanty. See, for example, Averil Cameron's *The Later Roman Empire: A.D. 284–430* (Cambridge, MA: Harvard University Press, 1993), pp. 141–43.

37. Ammianus Marcellinus, *History*, published as *The Later Roman Empire, A.D. 354–378*, trans. and ed. Walter Hamilton. New York: Penguin, 1986, pp. 411–12.

38. Ammianus, *History*, p. 435.

39. Quoted in Michael Grant, *The Roman Emperors*. New York: Barnes and Noble, 1997, p. 264.

40. Ferrill, *Fall of the Roman Empire*, pp. 84–85, 140.

41. Quoted in Simon Macdowall, *Late Roman Infantrymen, 236–565 A.D.* London: Osprey, 1994, p. 14.

42. A few scholars dispute that *plumbatae* were darts, suggesting instead that they may have been the heads of javelins.

43. Stewart Perowne, *The End of the Roman World*. New York: Thomas Y. Crowell, 1966, p. 21.

44. Pat Southern and Karen R. Dixon, *The Late Roman Army*. New Haven, CT: Yale University Press, 1996, p. 55.

Glossary

agrimensores: Surveyors.

alae sociorum: "Wings of allies"; in Rome's republican army, legions and other units composed of noncitizen allies.

aquilifer: A soldier who bore his legion's eagle (the *aquila*) and other standards.

as (plural *asses*): A copper coin worth ¼ of a *sestertius*.

auxilia: Military forces, consisting of noncitizens recruited from the provinces, that supplemented the regular Roman legions.

berm: In a fort, castle, or defensive fortification, the space between the moat and the outer wall.

carpentarii: Carpenters.

centuries: Small units within a Roman legion, at first containing a hundred men each and later containing eighty men each; a naval century consisted of the crew of one warship.

centurion: The lowest ranking senior officer who commanded a century. Considered to be the backbone of the army.

circumvallation: A basic siege technique consisting of surrounding a town or fortress with troops and fortifications, so that none of the besieged can escape and no one can get in to reinforce or supply them.

cohort (*cohors*): A unit of a Roman army legion, usually consisting of about five hundred men, used in the late Republic and thereafter until Rome's last two centuries.

cohortes urbanae: "Urban cohorts"; Rome's police force, instituted by the emperor Augustus.

comitatenses: In the Later Empire, mobile armies stationed in towns.

comitatus: In the Later Empire, the emperor's traveling court.

consul: In the Roman Republic, one of two jointly serving elected chief government administrators, who also commanded the armies; their office was the consulship, and matters pertaining to it or them were termed consular.

corvus: "Crow" or "raven"; a naval warfare device, consisting of a wooden gangway with a spike protruding from the end, which stood upright on a Roman deck until dropped onto an enemy deck. The spike penetrated the deck and held the ships together while Roman soldiers ran across and boarded the other vessel.

cuirass: Chest armor.

denarius (plural *denarii*): A silver coin worth ⅟₂₅ of an *aureas* (a common gold coin).

equites: "Knights"; Roman businessmen and other well-to-do individuals who comprised a non-land-based aristocracy second in prestige only to the landowning patricians; also, the cavalrymen drawn from this class.

forum: A city's main square, used for public gatherings and as a marketplace; also, the marketplace of a Roman army camp.

garrison: A group of soldiers manning a fort or other installation.

gladius: The short sword wielded by Roman soldiers.

gubernator: A Roman naval officer in charge of a ship's steersmen.

harpax: A grapnel (hook) hurled at an enemy ship by a catapult mounted on the deck of a Roman ship, with the object of holding fast the other ship so that it could be boarded.

hastati: In Rome's mid-republican army, young soldiers who fought in the first line of infantry.

hoplite: A heavily armored infantry soldier who fought in the phalanx formation.

immunis (plural *immunes*): A soldier who was excused (and therefore immune) from normal daily military duties because he possessed a special skill.

lapidarii: Stonemasons.

legatus: "Legate"; in the mid to late Republic, an officer in command of one or more legions.

legatus legionis: "Legionary legate"; from Augustus's time on, a military officer in command of a single legion.

legion: An army battalion, consisting at first of about 3,000 men, then about 4,200, and later about 5,000 or more.

legionary: An ordinary Roman soldier.

librarii: Clerks.

Liburnians (*liburnae*): Small, fast, highly maneuverable warships used by the Romans, especially in their provincial fleets.

limes: Frontier zones or borders.

limitanei: In the Later Empire, troops stationed on the frontiers.

magister equitum: "Master of cavalry"; in the Later Empire, the commander of the horsemen of a mobile army.

magister peditum: "Master of infantry"; in the Later Empire, the commander of the foot soldiers of a mobile army.

maniple: A tactical fighting unit, usually consisting of about 120 men, used in Rome's early and mid-republican armies.

manipular tactic: A basic combination of battlefield maneuvers in which the Roman maniples formed lines, each of which engaged in a separate charge against the enemy.

navarch: The commander of a Roman naval squadron.

oligarchy: A government controlled by a small elite group of individuals.

optio: A Roman army sergeant who was second in command to a centurion.

patricians: Landowners who comprised Rome's wealthiest and most privileged class.

Pax Romana: "Roman Peace"; the highly peaceful and prosperous era initiated by Augustus, lasting from about 30 B.C. to about A.D. 180.

phalanx: A battle formation introduced by the Greeks and adopted by the early Romans. Ranks (lines) of infantry soldiers stood one behind the other, their upraised shields and thrusting spears creating a formidable barrier.

pilum: A throwing spear (javelin).

plumbata: A lead-weighted dart thrown or slung by soldiers in the Later Empire.

portcullis: A heavy door made of wood and iron. Raised and lowered by ropes and winches, it protected the gate of a fortress or wall.

primus pilus: "First spear"; the highest-ranking centurion in a Roman legion.

principes: In Rome's mid-republican army, soldiers in the prime of their life, who fought in the second line of infantry.

quincunx: The pattern of dots displayed for the number five on dice cubes; also used to describe the checkerboard arrangement of the Roman maniples on the battlefield during republican times.

quinquereme: A warship likely having three banks of oars, with two men to an oar in the upper two banks and one man to an oar in the lowest bank.

sagitarii: Arrow makers.

scholae: In the Later Empire, cavalry forces guarding the emperor's traveling court.

scutum: A Roman legionary's originally oval and later rectangular shield. In the third century A.D., the *scutum* was abandoned as oval shields once more came into general use.

Senate: The Roman legislative branch, made up of well-to-do aristocrats. It directed foreign policy, advised the consuls, and in general controlled the state during the Republic.

sestertius (plural *sestertii* or *sesterces*): A silver or bronze coin originally equal to 2.5 *asses* and later 4, and also ¼ of a *denarius.*

signifer: A soldier who bore his century's standards.

spatha: A long sword wielded by infantry soldiers in the Later Empire.

spiculum: The most common throwing spear used by Roman soldiers in the Later Empire, it was similar to the older *pilum.*

standards: The emblems, flags, or colors of an army or army unit, usually raised on a pole as a rallying point for the soldiers.

stipendium: A soldier's pay.

tesserarius: A sort of low-ranking sergeant who made sure the Roman legionaries were doing their jobs.

triarii: In Rome's mid-republican army, older veterans who fought in the third line of infantry.

tribune (*tribunus*): "Tribal officer"; one of the six elected officers who ran an army legion; they ranked below a legate but above a centurion.

trierarch: The captain of a Roman warship.

trireme: A warship having three banks of oars, with one man to each oar.

velites: In Rome's mid-republican army, light-armed skirmishers who threw javelins at the enemy and then retreated behind the infantry.

veterinarii: Veterinarians; their facility within a Roman army camp was the *veterinarium.*

vigiles: Firefighters who doubled as night police, a paramilitary force introduced by Augustus for the city of Rome.

For Further Reading

Isaac Asimov, *The Roman Empire*. Boston: Houghton Mifflin, 1967. A fine, clearly written general overview of the main events of the Empire, including various battles and other highlights of Roman warfare.

Phil R. Cox and Annabel Spenceley, *Who Were the Romans?* New York: EDC Publications, 1994. An impressive, well-illustrated introduction to the Romans, presented in a question-and-answer format and aimed at basic readers.

Jill Hughes, *Imperial Rome*. New York: Gloucester Press, 1985. This nicely illustrated introduction to the Roman Empire will appeal to grade school readers.

Anthony Marks and Graham Tingay, *The Romans*. London: Usborne, 1990. An excellent summary of the main aspects of Roman history, life, and arts, supported by hundreds of beautiful and accurate drawings reconstructing Roman times. Aimed at basic readers but highly recommended for anyone interested in Roman civilization.

Don Nardo, *The Roman Republic* and *The Roman Empire*, San Diego: Lucent Books, 1994; *The Age of Augustus*, San Diego: Lucent Books, 1996; *Greek and Roman Mythology* and *Life in Ancient Rome*, San Diego: Lucent Books, 1997; *Life of a Roman Slave*, San Diego: Lucent Books, 1998; and *The Ancient Romans*, San Diego: Lucent Books, 2000. These comprehensive but easy-to-read volumes provide an overview of Roman life and history for junior high and high school readers (as well as ambitious younger readers).

Jonathan Rutland, *See Inside a Roman Town*. New York: Barnes and Noble, 1986. A very attractively illustrated introduction to some major concepts of Roman civilization for basic readers.

Judith Simpson, *Ancient Rome*. New York: Time-Life Books, 1997. One of the latest entries in Time-Life's library of picture books about the ancient world, this one is beautifully illustrated with attractive and appropriate photographs and paintings. The general but well-written text is aimed at intermediate young readers.

Major Works Consulted

Modern Sources

M.C. Bishop and J.C. Coulston, *Roman Military Equipment*. Princes Risborough, England: Shire Publications, 1989. A very useful summary of Roman arms and other military materials.

Lionel Casson, *The Ancient Mariners: Seafarers and Sea Fighters of the Mediterranean in Ancient Times*. Princeton, NJ: Princeton University Press, 1991. This enduring and popular book by a fine classical scholar contains several useful chapters on Roman ships, including warships. Casson includes a number of English translations of letters written by Roman sailors.

Peter Connolly, *Greece and Rome at War*. London: Macdonald, 1998. A highly informative and useful volume by one of the finest historians of ancient military affairs. Connolly, whose stunning paintings adorn this and his other books, is also the foremost modern illustrator of the an-

cient world. Highly recommended.

Arther Ferrill, *The Fall of the Roman Empire: The Military Explanation*. New York: Thames and Hudson, 1986. In this excellent work, written in a straightforward style, Ferrill supports the position that Rome fell mainly because its army grew increasingly less disciplined and formidable in the Empire's last two centuries, while at the same time the overall defensive strategy of the emperors was ill conceived and contributed to the ultimate fall.

Edward Gibbon, *The Decline and Fall of the Roman Empire*. First published 1776–1788. Among the better modern editions are a seven-volume version edited by the noted historian J.B. Bury (London: Methuen, 1909–1914; later published in three volumes—New York: Heritage Press, 1946), and a three-volume version edited by David Womersley (New York: Penguin, 1994). Gibbon's masterwork contains a wealth of material about the Roman army's legions, leaders, campaigns, and battles. Bury and Womersley provide commentary updating Gibbon's information in light of discoveries made since his time.

Michael Grant, *The Army of the Caesars*. New York: M. Evans, 1974. A very informative volume that examines the evolving Roman army from the days of Marius in the late Republic to the much inferior Roman military machine of the Later Empire.

Sir John Hackett, ed., *Warfare in the Ancient World*. New York: Facts On File, 1989. An excellent analysis of the weapons, siege devices, and military customs and strategies of the major ancient cultures, each covered by a world-class historian. The sections on Rome include "The Early Roman Army" and "The Roman Army of the Age of Polybius," by Peter Connolly; "The Roman Army of the Later Republic," by Lawrence Keppie (author of *The Making of the Roman Army;* see below); "The Empire," by Brian Dobson; and "The Late-Roman Empire," by Roger Tomlin.

Lawrence Keppie, *The Making of the Roman Army: From Republic to Empire*. New York: Barnes and Noble, 1984. Keppie, a noted scholar and archaeologist, begins with a fine overview of Rome's early military development, then goes into considerable detail on Roman soldiers, military equipment, and bat-tles in the late Republic and early Empire.

Simon Macdowall, *Late Roman Infantrymen, 236–565 A.D.* London: Osprey, 1994. This well-illustrated volume offers a detailed look at how Roman infantrymen dressed, trained, marched, and fought in the Empire's last precarious centuries.

Kurt Raaflaub and Nathan Rosenstein, eds., *War and Society in the Ancient and Medieval Worlds*. Cambridge, MA: Harvard University Press, 1999. An excellent collection of essays by noted military historians, each summarizing the basic approach to and methods of warfare by an ancient people. The essay on republican Rome is by Rosenstein, of Ohio State University at Columbus; the one on imperial Rome is by Brian Campbell, of Queen's University of Belfast.

Nick Sekunda, *The Roman Army, 200–104 B.C.* London: Osprey, 1996. This nicely illustrated volume by a highly respected scholar goes into great detail about Roman army personnel, uniforms, weapons, and tactics in the transitional period of the second century B.C., including the major changes made by Marius in 107–104 B.C. A must for military buffs.

Michael Simkins, *The Roman Army from Caesar to Trajan: An Illustrated Military History of the Roman Legions*. London: Osprey, 1984. The weapons, uniforms, camps, and battle tactics of Roman soldiers during the early Empire are highlighted in this nicely illustrated volume.

Pat Southern and Karen R. Dixon, *The Late Roman Army*. New Haven, CT: Yale University Press, 1996. This well-written, scholarly volume examines the gradual, nearly three-century-long decline of the Roman army, beginning with the events of the "century of crisis" (the third century B.C.). Included are illuminating sections on weapons factories, fortifications, siege warfare, and troop morale.

G.R. Watson, *The Roman Soldier*. London: Thames and Hudson, 1969. One of the better of the many books on the Roman army, this one contains much detailed information about how the troops were recruited, their training, pay, weapons, camps, and so on.

Graham Webster, *The Roman Imperial Army*. Totowa, NJ: Barnes and Noble, 1985. A distinguished former University of Birmingham scholar, Webster delivers an information-packed study of the army as it evolved during the Empire. Includes very useful chapters on frontier systems, camps and forts, and peaceful activities engaged in by the soldiers.

Terence Wise, *Armies of the Carthaginian Wars, 265–146 B.C.* London: Osprey, 1996. Another handsome and useful book in Osprey's series on ancient warfare, this one concentrates on the Roman military during the epic Punic Wars, in which Rome squared off against the powerful maritime empire of Carthage.

Ancient Sources

Ammianus Marcellinus, *History*, published as *The Later Roman Empire, A.D. 354–378*. Trans. and ed. Walter Hamilton. New York: Penguin, 1986.

Kenneth J. Atchity, ed., *The Classical Greek Reader*. New York: Oxford University Press, 1996.

Julius Caesar, *Commentaries on the Gallic Wars* and *Commentaries on the Civil Wars*, published as *War Commentaries of Caesar*. Trans. Rex Warner. New York: New American Library, 1960.

Dio Cassius, *Roman History*, published as *The Roman History: The Reign of Augustus*. Trans. Ian Scott-Kilvert. New York: Penguin, 1987.

Dionysius of Halicarnassus, *Roman Antiquities*. 7 vols. Trans. Earnest Cary. Cambridge, MA: Harvard University Press, 1963.

Josephus, *The Jewish War*. Trans. G.A. Williamson; rev. E. Mary Smallwood. New York: Penguin, 1970, 1981.

Naphtali Lewis and Meyer Reinhold, eds., *Roman Civilization, Sourcebook I: The Republic*, and *Roman Civilization, Sourcebook II: The Empire*. New York: Harper and Row, 1966.

Livy, *The History of Rome from Its Foundation*. Books 1–5 published as *Livy: The Early History of Rome*. Trans.

117

Aubrey de Sélincourt. New York: Penguin, 1971; books 21–30 published as *Livy: The War with Hannibal*. Trans. Aubrey de Sélincourt. New York: Penguin, 1972; books 31–45 published as *Livy: Rome and the Mediterranean*. Trans. Henry Bettenson. New York: Penguin, 1976.

Plutarch, *Parallel Lives*, excerpted in *Fall of the Roman Republic: Six Lives by Plutarch*. Trans. Rex Warner. New York: Penguin, 1972; and *Makers of Rome: Nine Lives by Plutarch*. Trans. Ian Scott-Kilvert. New York: Penguin, 1965.

Polybius, *The Histories*. Trans. Ian Scott-Kilvert. New York: Penguin, 1979.

Additional Works Consulted

Lesley Adkins and Roy A. Adkins, *Handbook to Life in Ancient Rome*. New York: Facts On File, 1994.

Paul G. Bahn, ed., *The Cambridge Illustrated History of Archaeology*. New York: Cambridge University Press, 1996.

Gavin de Beer, *Hannibal: Challenging Rome's Supremacy*. New York: Viking Press, 1969.

Arthur E.R. Boak, *Manpower Shortage and the Fall of the Roman Empire in the West*. 1955; reprint, Westport, CT: Greenwood Press, 1974.

Peter Brown, *The World of Late Antiquity, A.D. 150–750*. New York: Harcourt Brace, 1971.

J.B. Bury, *History of the Later Roman Empire, 395–565*, 2 vols. New York: Dover, 1957.

———, *The Invasion of Europe by the Barbarians*. New York: Norton, 1967.

Averil Cameron, *The Later Roman Empire: A.D. 284–430*. Cambridge, MA: Harvard University Press, 1993.

Lionel Casson, *Daily Life in Ancient Rome*. New York: American Heritage, 1975.

Brian Caven, *The Punic Wars*. New York: Barnes and Noble, 1992.

T.J. Cornell, *The Beginnings of Rome*. London: Routledge, 1995.

Tim Cornell and John Matthews, *Atlas of the Roman World*. New York: Facts On File, 1982.

Michael Crawford, *The Roman Republic*. Cambridge, MA: Harvard University Press, 1992.

Roy W. Davies, *Service in the Roman Army*. Ed. David Breeze and Valerie A. Maxfield. New York: Columbia University Press, 1989.

Walter Goffart, *Barbarians and Romans, A.D. 418–584: The Techniques of Accommodation*. Princeton, NJ: Princeton University Press, 1980.

Michael Grant, *Caesar*. London: Weidenfeld and Nicolson, 1974.

———, *The Fall of the Roman Empire*. New York: Macmillan, 1990.

———, *History of Rome*. New York: Scribner's, 1978.

————, *The Roman Emperors.* New York: Barnes and Noble, 1997.

P.A. Holder, *The Roman Army in Britain.* London: Batsford, 1982.

A.H.M. Jones, *Constantine and the Conversion of Europe.* Toronto: University of Toronto Press, 1979.

————, *The Later Roman Empire, 284–602.* 3 vols, 1964; reprint, Norman: University of Oklahoma Press, 1975.

Archer Jones, *The Art of War in the Western World.* New York: Oxford University Press, 1987.

John Keegan, *A History of Warfare.* New York: Random House, 1993.

Phillip A. Kildahl, *Gaius Marius.* New York: Twayne, 1968.

J.F. Lazenby, *The First Punic War: A Military History.* Stanford: Stanford University Press, 1996.

Edward N. Luttwak, *The Grand Strategy of the Roman Empire.* Baltimore: Johns Hopkins University Press, 1976.

Ramsay MacMullen, *Roman Government's Response to Crisis: A.D. 235–337.* New Haven, CT: Yale University Press, 1976.

E.W. Marsden, *Greek and Roman Artillery.* Oxford: Clarendon Press, 1969.

Valerie A. Maxfield, *The Military Decorations of the Roman Army.* London: Batsford, 1981.

Stewart Perowne, *The End of the Roman World.* New York: Thomas Y. Crowell, 1966.

Justine Davis Randers-Pehrson, *Barbarians and Romans: The Birth Struggle of Europe, A.D. 400–700.* Norman: University of Oklahoma Press, 1983.

Boris Rankov, *Guardians of the Roman Empire.* London: Osprey, 1994.

W.L. Rodgers, *Greek and Roman Naval Warfare.* Annapolis, MD: Naval Institute Press, 1964.

Michael Simkins, *Warriors of Rome: An Illustrated History of the Roman Legions.* London: Blandford, 1988.

Chester G. Starr, *The Influence of Sea Power on Ancient History.* New York: Oxford University Press, 1989.

————, *The Roman Imperial Navy, 31 B.C.–A.D. 324.* Ithaca, NY: Cornell University Press, 1941. 2nd ed., Cambridge: Heffe, 1960.

Sidney Toy, *Castles: Their Construction and History.* New York: Dover, 1984.

F.W. Walbank, *The Awful Revolution: The Decline of the Roman Empire in the West.* Toronto: University of Toronto Press, 1969.

John Warry, *Warfare in the Classical World.* Norman: University of Oklahoma Press, 1995.

Index

Actium (battle), 39, 51

admirals, 85

   see also navy

Adrianople (battle), 94–96

Agrigentum, 68

Agrippa, Marcus, 51, 85

Alani, 93

Alesia (fortress), 69–72

Allia (battle), 25–27, 28

Ambrose (Christian bishop), 95

Ammianus, Marcellinus, 95

amphitheater, 66, 67

Antoninus Pius (Roman emperor), 63, 88

Antony, Mark, 45, 51, 76

armor, 46, 97–98

   see also clothing

army

   archers, 48, 85

   artillery, 71, 72

   barracks, 65

   bodyguards, 44, 55

   brutality of, 11–12

   camps, 64–65

   cavalry, 15, 22, 46, 91

   centuries, 15, 30

   centurions, 45, 49, 65–66, 86

   discipline of, 11, 89, 98, 100

   drills, 52, 89, 98, 100

   hoplites, 16, 17, 20

   infantry, 17, 31

   leadership of, 49, 88–90

   mobility of, 92

   officers, 45, 49, 51

   organization of, 11, 33, 99

   pay for, 45

   phalanx, 20–23, 24, 28, 39

   salaries for, 45

   skirmishers, 29

   slingers, 46

   training, 51–54, 92

   tribunes, 15, 49

   see also battle tactics; clothing; weapons

assassinations, 57

assault. *See* siege warfare

Augustus (Roman emperor), 46, 50, 60, 80, 88

Averni (or Arverni), 68

barbarians, 89–90, 91, 93

barbarization, 96–99

bathhouses, 65, 66–67

battle formations, 20–23, 28, 36, 53

battle tactics, 31, 36, 55, 99

ben Ya'ir, Eleazar, 73

blockades, 69
   see also siege warfare

Britain, 55, 60

Byzantine Empire, 100

Caerleon, 67

Caesar, Julius, 45, 51, 69–71

Caligula (Roman emperor), 57

Camillus, Marcus Furius, 28

Cannae (battle), 33, 35–38

Cape Echnomus (naval battle) 84

Caracella (Roman emperor), 45

Carnantum, 66

Carthage, 12, 33, 75, 78

Carthaginians, 33, 35–39, 84

Casson, Lionel, 75–76, 82–83

catapults, 71, 85
   see also siege warfare

cavalry, 15, 22, 46, 91

ceremonies, 21–22, 39

charge, 31

Christianity, 100

circumvallation, 68–69
   see also siege warfare

city-state, 44

class system, 23–24
   see also patricians

Claudius (Roman emperor), 57

Cleopatra VII (queen of Egypt), 45, 51

clothing
   armor, 17, 18–20, 30–31
   baldric (belt), 99
   cuirass (breastplate), 17, 55–56, 57
   greave (leg protector), 17, 31
   helmet, 17–18, 29, 31
   mail, 46
   shield, 18–19, 20, 28, 57

cohorts, 46
   see also urban cohorts

Colosseum, 67, 77

Commentaries on the Gallic Wars
   (Caesar), 69–71

Commodus (Roman emperor), 57

Connolly, Peter, 20, 31, 41–42, 60, 69, 85

conquests. *See* Roman civilization, conquests

conscription, 99–100

Constantine I (Roman emperor), 91, 92

Constantinople, 100

consuls, 33, 49

Corinth, 12

corvus (naval device), 79, 83, 84, 85

crewmen. *See* sailors

cuirass, 31

Cynoscephalae (battle), 40–42

Danube River, 63

decline. *See* Roman civilization, decline of

desertion, from military, 92

Dio Cassius, 39

Diocletian (Roman emperor), 63, 90, 91, 92

discipline, 89, 98, 100

ditches, 63, 64

Dixon, Karen, 99, 101

Dobson, Brian, 62–63

Domitian (Roman emperor), 45

draft. *See* conscription

elephants, 40, 42

Etruscans, 15, 16–17, 25

Ferrill, Arther, 90

firefighters, 58–59

Flamininus, Titus Quinctius, 40

Flavius Silva, 73

formations. *See* battle formations

fortifications, 38–39, 60, 63, 64, 68

fortresses. *See* fortifications

forts. *See* fortifications

forum, 66

Franks, 93, 98

Gaiseric, 96

Gallic Wars, 68–72

Gallienus (Roman emperor), 91, 92

gangways, 83, 85
    see also naval tactics

garrisons, 38–39
    see also fortifications

Gauls, 25–27, 68

Germans, 89, 91, 99–100

gladiator fights, 67

gods and goddesses, 82

Goths, 93, 94–95

Grant, Michael, 13

grapnel (hooks), 85
    see also naval tactics

Greeks, 33

Hadrian (Roman emperor), 60, 88

Hadrian's Wall, 62–63

Hannibal, 33, 35–37

horsemen. *See* cavalry

Huns, 93–94

immunes (Roman officers), 49

infantry, 17, 31

Isis, 82

Jerusalem, 74

Josephus, 72

Judaea, 72

Keppie, Lawrence, 24, 40

knights, 16

Late Roman Army, The (Southern and Dixon), 99, 101

Latins, 14–15, 22

legate, 49

legionary, 45, 49

legions, 15–16, 33

Liburnian, 81–82
Livy, 22, 23, 26–27

Macedonians, 39, 40–42
Macedonian Wars, 39–42
mail, 46, 97–98
maneuvers. *See* battle formations; battle tactics; naval maneuvers; naval tactics
maniples, 28, 29–33
manipular system, 28, 29–33
Marcellinus, Ammianus, 93–94
Marcus Aurelius (emperor of Rome), 88
Marius, Gaius, 44, 45, 46
Masada, 73, 74
Mediterranean Sea, 42
military bases. *See* fortifications
militia, 15
missile throwers, 71, 72
moats, 65
Monarchy, 10, 15, 24

naval maneuvers, 82–85
naval officers, 85–86
naval tactics, 82–85
navy, 39, 75–77, 85, 86–87
Neptune, 82
Nereus, 82
Nero (emperor of Rome), 59
Nerva (emperor of Rome), 88
Notitia Dignitiatum (list of Roman officials), 95

oarsmen, 76, 81, 86–87
    see also sailors
Octavian. *See* Augustus
Odoacer (Roman commander), 101

Palatine Hill, 55
Palestine, 72
patricians, 15, 24
Paullus, Lucius Aemilius, 41
Pax Romana (Roman Peace), 60, 80, 88
Perowne, Stewart, 99–100
Perseus (Macedonian king), 41
Pertinax (Roman emperor), 57
phalanx, 20–23, 24, 28, 39
Philip V (Macedonian king), 40
Phoenicians, 75
pirates, 77, 81–82
Plutarch, 46
policemen, 58–59
Polybius, 12, 31, 37–38, 51–52, 75, 78–79
portcullis, 61–62
Praetorian Guard, 55, 57
Punic Wars, 33, 35–39, 68–69, 76, 79, 84
Pydna (battle), 41, 42

quadrireme, 80, 81
quinquereme, 80, 81

ramming, 82
ramparts, 64
ramps, 72, 73

"raven." *See corvus*

Republic, 10, 24, 44

Rhine River, 63

rituals, 21–22, 39

roads, 63

Roman civilization

  administrative caliber of, 13

  borders of, 63

  conquests and, 11, 22, 33, 34, 35, 43

  decline of, 88–90, 92, 96–100

  duration of, 10

  political management skills of, 13

  war as important component of, 10–11

Roman History, The: The Reign of Augustus (Dio Cassius), 39

Rome

  city-state beginnings of, 15–16

  class structure of, 15, 23–24

  expansion of, 11, 22, 23, 24–27, 34, 43

  governmental forms of, 10, 15, 24

  location of, 14–15

  see also firefighters; Latins; policemen

Romulus, 22, 60

Romulus Augustulanus (Roman emperor), 101

Rosenstein, Nathan, 37

rowers. *See* oarsmen

Sabines, 22

sailors, 75–77, 85, 86–87

  see also naval tactics; navy

Samnites, 33, 34

Scipio, Publius Cornelius, 38

Seleucia, 39

Senate, 15, 24, 44

senators, 85

Servian Wall, 61

Servius Tullius, 23

shields, 18–19, 20, 28, 57

ships. *See* warships

Sicily, 78, 84

siege warfare, 60, 67, 68–74

Simkins, Michael, 55

Southern, Pat, 99, 101

stockades, 63

"stone caster," 71

strategy, 55

swords, 99

tactics. *See* battle tactics; naval tactics

Tacticus, Aeneas, 61–62

Taras (battle), 77

Tiberius (Roman emperor), 57

Titus (Roman emperor), 74

Trajan (Roman emperor), 55, 88, 90

triremes, 80–81

Triton, 82

uniform. *See* clothing

urban cohorts, 58

Valens (Roman emperor), 94–95

Vandals, 93, 96

Vegetius, 52, 54

Veii, 25

Vercingetorix, 68

vigiles (firefighters and policemen), 58

Vindolanda, 68

Visigoths, 94

walls, 60–63

War and Society in the Ancient and Medieval Worlds (Rosenstein), 37

Warry, John, 21

warships, 76–82

watchtowers, 63, 64

weapons, 98

ax, 20, 98

bow and arrow, 98

dagger, 20

darts, 99

javelin, 20, 31, 98

pike, 39

spear, 19, 28

sword, 18, 20, 31, 99

Webster, Graham, 66

Picture Credits

About the Author

Historian Don Nardo has written numerous volumes about ancient Rome, including *Life of a Roman Slave*, *The Age of Augustus*, *Rulers of Ancient Rome*, and Greenhaven Press's massive *Encyclopedia of Ancient Rome*. He is also the editor of *Classical Greece and Rome*, the second volume of the ten-part World History by Era series. Mr. Nardo resides with his wife, Christine, in Massachusetts.